Linda Kearns
A Revolutionary Irish Woman

Linda Kearns
A Revolutionary Irish Woman

Proinnsíos Ó Duigneáin

Drumlin Publications

First published in 2002 by
Drumlin Publications,
Nure, Manorhamilton, Co. Leitrim, Ireland.
072-55237

© Proinnsíos Ó Duigneáin

All rights reserved. No part of this book may be reprinted or reproduced or transmitted in any form without the prior permission of the publishers.

ISBN: 1 873437 26 9

Design: Red Eye
Printed by: Colour Books, Dublin

Contents

Acknowledgements 6

Introduction 8

Illustrations 64 & 128

Chapter One Home & Early Life 11

Chapter Two Active Service 1916-1920 20

Chapter Three Capture 36

Chapter Four Imprisonment 44

Chapter Five Escape and Civil War 59

Chapter Six America & Australia 1922-25 71

Chapter Seven Fianna Fail 98

Chapter Eight Charles McWhinney & Marriage 107

Chapter Nine Nursing Issues 123

Chapter Ten Visiting Committee 136

Chapter Eleven Women's Industrial Development Association W.I.D.A. 143

Chapter Twelve Kilrock 156

References 166

Bibliography 176

Index 180

Acknowledgements

I owe a deep debt of gratitude to the many people who assisted my research into this life of Linda Kearns. I am especially grateful to those who shared their memories of her with me. Since Linda left no personal papers it would have been impossible to build up a picture without their knowledge and insight. First mention must be made of those who sadly have passed away since work on the project began: Séamus Mulligan, Linda's nephew, who was generous with his time in Dublin and Sligo; Sheila Clarke whose views were conveyed with commendable directness; Mary Creed, Dromahaire, who gave me vital information about a period that would otherwise have been neglected. Sonas síoraí dóibh.

I am especially grateful to Mary Duffy (née Kearns) for her assistance and indeed for her hospitality and to Mary's daughter Delia McDevitt who initiated the project.

Damian MacGarry, Linda's grandnephew provided family and other details many of which came via his father Bernard (R.I.P.).

Séamus Clarke supplied me with valuable information not alone on Linda's family and her native place but also on aspects of her life in Dublin where he himself lived for a number of years.

Táim thar a bheith buíoch de Annraoi Ó Beoláin a thug cead dom dialann a aintín, Kathleen Boland, agus páipéir eile a léamh.

Thank you to Josie Torsney, Tomás Ó Duibhir, Kate McGinley, Michael Crawford, Kathleen Mawn, Margaret Galloway, (R.I.P.), and Margaret Vanek.

I benefited from the assistance of the following historians, national and local: Máire Mac Domhnaill-Gairbhí, Michael Farry, Joe McGowan, Harry Bradshaw, Jim Maher and especially Maria Luddy and Gerard McAtasney.

My thanks to the following: the staff of the National Archives, Bishop Street especially Tom Quinlan; Séamus

Helferty in the U.C.D. archives; Victor Laing in the Military Archives; the staff of the Public Record Office, Kew, London; Niamh Adams of The Irish Nurses' Organisation Library, Fitzwilliam Place; Catherine Harrison and Aoife MacEoin of The Irish Red Cross, Merrion Square; the library staff of An Bord Altranais; the staff of Sligo Co. Library and Mary O'Doherty of Mercer's Library.

A special word of gratitude to Theresa Kelly, Mae Kelly, Mary Corby and Seán Ó Súilleabháin of Co. Leitrim Library. I also wish to acknowledge my indebtedness to Ann Coughlan, Co. Librarian, Tullamore, Co. Offaly.

My greatest debt of gratitude are to the following: Linda's daughter Ann whose information on every period of her mother's life was vital for the writing of this book. Her press cuttings of her mother's fund-raising mission in America and other documents were invaluable; Martina Kearns who assiduously sought out information which would otherwise have been quite difficult for me to obtain; Aoife, my daughter who spent hours in the Public Record Office in London locating documents on the War of Independence period which meant a considerable saving on the time I myself had to spend in Kew; Betty, my wife whose technical expertise in type-setting and layout speeded up the process in the final stages of the work.

Introduction

Linda Kearns is representative of a number of women of the first half of the 20th century who played significant but largely unacknowledged roles in the 1916-1921 period in Ireland and who later were active in trying to influence the direction of politics in the fledgling state. She was not a letter writer, she did not keep a diary and she left no significant body of papers. Nevertheless this research has brought to light for the writer and hopefully for the reader a career as a revolutionary and public figure which was productive, certainly varied and often attended by danger and risk-taking.

Linda is recognised for her involvement in the War of Independence and for her subsequent capture, imprisonment and daring escape from Mountjoy Prison in 1921. Not as well known was her lifelong mission to achieve greater rights for the nursing profession of which she herself was a member. Indeed one of the most striking aspects of her life was the wide range of issues in which she became involved. These include conditions in prisons and the lot of prisoners, the plight of refugees and of other victims of the Second World War, the rights of women in general and of nurses in particular. Her work as a promoter of native industry has gone largely unrecorded. Politically, she took the anti-Treaty side and went abroad on two major fund-raising campaigns for the republican side. Later she threw in her lot with Fianna Fáil and was voted onto the first executive of that party in 1926, a position she retained almost until her death. Her relationship with de Valera's party was at times an uneasy one especially in the wake of legislation passed in the mid-1930s.

Like many successful women of her time her personal circumstances facilitated an active role in public life. The fact that she was bequeathed a substantial sum of money when she was still quite young putting her in 'the person of private means' category, meant that she could pursue her objectives with comparative ease. She did not marry until late in life and her women friends such as Máire Comerford and especially Dorothy Macardle provided constant support. Yet Linda had her own personal traumas; the break-up of her marriage; the life threatening illness of her only child; the deaths at relatively young ages of many of her family and the loss of friends who fought with her in the War of Independence and the Civil War.

Now over fifty years after her death, her memory lives in the minds of the few still alive who knew her. The freshness of that memory owes as much to her kindness and great personal charm as it does to the record of her exploits. By nature she was outgoing. She travelled widely, in Europe, America and Australia. She was an inveterate smoker disposing of upwards of sixty Goldflake cigarettes a day. Woodbines, in her opinion, were a superior brand except that 'they were too bloody small!' She had no hesitation in smoking or taking a whiskey at the open bar of a pub. Not for her the clandestine drink in the snug as was the practice of some women of her time. She owned and drove her own car before and during the Troubles. Although reared on a small farm she was middle class in outlook. Many who knew her would say that she was confident but not arrogant, decisive but not overbearing. She was intelligent but was not an intellectual. One commentator wrote at the time of her death about her great ability as a knitter and needle woman, talents which she perfected during long hours of night duty as a nurse. Another commented simply that 'there was great stuff in her.'

Chapter One
Home & Early Life

In her prime of life Linda Kearns was a tall woman, about five feet ten, and of slender build. One acquaintance described her as 'wiry'[1] and everyone commented on her very dark brown eyes. She had prominent front teeth which she usually concealed with her upper lip when photographs were being taken. She walked with long strides and seemed to be always in a hurry. By all accounts she had a very pleasant demeanour with a ready smile. In the last few years of her life, although still a relatively young woman, she became somewhat stooped.

She was born in the townland of Cloonagh, parish of Dromard, Co. Sligo. Her father, Thomas Kearns was a small farmer, with just over twenty seven acres.[2] According to family sources, he was 'an upstanding loyalist man from whom she certainly did not get her republicanism.'[3] Her mother Catherine Clarke was born and reared next door to her future husband. Linda attended Ballacutranta national school where she was taught by her aunt, her mother's sister, Honora Kelly (née Clarke) of Port Royal, in the girls' section. The boys' section was taught by Honora's brother James Clarke, N.T. James also surveyed land for the local landlord Malby Crofton of Longford House and for a time he was a tutor to the Crofton children. Another brother, Thomas Clarke, became a prominent politician in Dun Laoghaire, and he was to play an important role in the fortunes of the Kearns' family. Linda's maternal grandmother was Maria Cunlisk from Dromahaire, Co. Leitrim, a native Irish speaker[4] while her maternal grandfather was 'well versed in classical lore and in the theory and practice of growing roots'. He was acquainted with Sydney Owenson, afterwards better known as Lady Morgan who wrote her novel *The Wild Irish Girl* when she resided with the Croftons in nearby Longford House. He often saw the 'famous little lady dance a four hand reel with Glorvina and others on the village green'. His brother, a priest, was at Killala when the French landed in 1798. Before ordination he had been educated at an excellent school in Ennis by a well known teacher of the time named Muldowney.[5]

Longford House was visited on a number of occasions by the famous harper, Turlough O'Carolan (1670-1738) who composed at least four tunes for members of the family one of which was written in praise of Elizabeth Robinson who married James Crofton c.1732. It is acknowledged as one of Carolan's best compositions. During the 1914-18 war Longford House was accidentally burned down. It appears that dried moss which was strewn on the ground floor caught fire from a lighted candle. This moss was used in the making of bandages for the wounded in the war.

Linda was born on 25 July and baptised on 1 August 1886.[6] However the name on the baptismal register is Brigid and years later she explained to her own daughter, Ann, the circumstances under which her name was changed to Belinda and thence Linda. Apparently for the first few years of her life she was known in the family as Beezie, a common variation at the time of Brigid. On her first day at school her aunt, the schoolmistress decided that 'no kin of hers' would have such a name as Beezie entered in the roll book. Instead she decided to call the child Belinda and 'it says much for the awe in which even the adults stood of the autocratic mistress that never again was Beezie heard of.'[7]

The baptismal register also reveals that Linda that was in fact three years older than the age she claimed she was during her adult life. For example she gave her age as twenty eight when she was imprisoned in 1920 whereas she was actually thirty four.[8] Her age, fifteen, is correctly recorded in the 1901 census where incidentally her name is written Belinda, not Brigid.[9] There were eight other children born to Thomas and Catherine Kearns. The eldest, Mary was born in 1869 and she was followed by Julia,

Annie, Thomas, who according to family tradition was handicapped and died in infancy, Michael, Kate, Sarah, and Nora. Michael contracted epilepsy and died in 1917. Sarah was more familiarly known as Daisy.[10]

In 1911, the Kearns' house in Cloonagh was described as thatched, with three rooms and three windows on the front. Thomas also had seven outhouses; a piggery, two cowhouses, a fowlhouse, a stable, a barn and a turfhouse. A servant, John Lucey, then aged sixteen, lived with the family. According to family sources, he was an orphan who had been brought to Cloonagh from Kerry by Mary, Linda's sister, after she had spent a period of time nursing there. The townland had a population of sixty eight of which eight were members of the Church of Ireland. Apart from Kearns, the other names were: Wynne, Maye, McCann, Farry, Harte, McLoughlin, Quinn, Clarke and Sproule.[11]

Linda's uncle, Thomas Clarke, the Dun Laoghaire politician, came to Dublin in 1868. He first became involved in the Home Rule Association founded by Isaac Butt. Later he was elected to the Rathdown Board of Guardians and became chairman in 1903. In that same year he had 'the unique distinction on the occasion of His Majesty's visit of being chairman of four public boards: the Rathdown Board of Guardians, the Blackrock Urban Council, Deans Grange Burial Board and the Port Sanitary Board.' In 1902, under his chairmanship, Deans Grange cemetery was extended by eight acres. He was also instrumental in having a Catholic and a Protestant chaplain appointed to the cemetery.[12] Thomas Clarke and his wife, formerly Alice Sexton, adopted Daisy the youngest of the Kearns children when she was very young. Daisy in later life resented having been taken from her home saying that they (her father and mother) 'had fed seven, they could have fed another'.[13] According to family sources, Thomas Clarke also helped the Kearns family financially. He was the owner of Trenton a substantial property in Ballsbridge, Dublin. Daisy inherited this property.[14]

Between April 1902 and September 1904, Linda and

Nora attended the Convent of the Blessed Virgin, Beirlegem, twenty miles north of Brussells in Belgium. It is most likely that the fees were paid by their uncle Thomas Clarke. A family source suggests that Linda's eldest sister, Mary may also have borne some of the expense since she was believed to have been left a sum of money by a patient she had nursed. There may be some confusion here between Mary and Linda who was a beneficiary of a will some fifteen years later. In any event Mary's according to the 1901 census was 'an unemployed lady's companion'. The local priest was also involved in setting up contact with the Belgium nuns.[15]

On the day they left for Belgium, Linda and Nora travelled by train with their father to Dublin where they were met by their uncle Thomas Clarke. The next stage of the journey was by boat to Holyhead. Waiting for them was one of the congregation of the Blessed Virgin who had come to escort the Irish and English students to the convent in Belgium. Later, on the train journey they were joined by Louisa Josephs from Northumberland.[16] In Beirlegem Linda received a good grounding in French which stood her in good stead in later life. Louisa A Josephs wrote the following in 1951 shortly after Linda's death: 'I am very proud to have been her school friend in the convent... We all loved her and her sister, dear Nora; they were such sweet, good tempered girls. Their progress in French, music and painting etc. was extraordinary! Sometimes in the dormitory when all the Belgian girls had gone home for the holidays, they would both dance some of the old Irish folk dances with great gusto and such happy high spirits; we little thought then what a serious, magnificent future lay in front of dear Bridgit. I was older than dear Linda as I am 70 years of age.'[17] It is interesting to note that Miss Josephs uses both names, Linda and Bridgit in her letter.

In 1907 Linda was accepted as a probationer nurse by the Royal City of Dublin Hospital, founded in 1831, and more commonly known as 'Baggot Street.' She was recommended by Lady Crofton of Longford House and she also had a reference from her aunt, the teacher, Mrs. Kelly.[18] Baggot Street's patrons were King Edward VII and the Lord Lieutenant of Ireland. Its vice-patrons included the Lord Mayor of Dublin; the Protestant Archbishop of Dublin; the Dean of St. Patricks; Lord Ardilaun; the Earl of Pembroke; and the Lord Chancellor. As part of her training Linda attended lectures in Anatomy, Ophthamology, Physiology, Hygiene, Medicine, Surgery and Gynaecology.[19] She proved to be a brilliant student securing first place and first class honours in both her primary and final examinations.[20] According to the minutes of the Nursing Committee she was awarded £1 for her success in the 1907 examination.[21] After her training period of three years she stayed on in Baggot Street for a further two years as a qualified nurse. First place in her final examination entitled her to receive six months training in a particular branch of nursing of her own choice. She elected to do massage. In later life she advocated the efficacy of this treatment for the relief of stiffness and even for the breaking up of phlegm in the chest of a patient suffering from flu or a heavy cold.[22]

In Baggot Street there were two types of probationers; articled and paying. The articled students had to pay a fee of £30 on enrolment and on completion of training were required to serve two more years in hospital, district or private nursing. 'All fees earned by them shall be the property of the Hospital and they are not allowed to receive gratuities. After four years, having passed the prescribed examinations, they become entitled, on the completion of four years from the date of entering the hospital, to a certificate of qualification.' The paying probationer's entrance fee was £70. It is not clear from the regulations what was the rate of pay subsequently.[23] In regard to Linda's status in Baggot Street it is probable that she was an articled probationer since she was over four years in the establishment. Incidentally, 'except under special circumstances', both types of probationers had to be between twenty one and thirty two years of age for admission as student nurses. If Linda was not treated as an exception, this stipulation would strengthen the view that she was born in 1886 and not 1889.

Life was tough for the student nurse in Baggot Street. She had little time off and very strict controls were operated by the Lady Superintendent. If there was a breach of discipline or some other indiscretion, the nurse was required to come before the Nursing Committee, a body which was comprised entirely of male members of the hospital staff. As regards salary she received £10 for her first year which rose to £18 for the fourth year. She was entitled to one month's holidays in the year and she had her own bedroom in the Nurses Home, the foundation stone of which was laid by Princess Christian of Schleswig-Holstein in 1900. In the same year Queen Victoria decreed that in future the hospital would be known as the Royal City of Dublin Hospital.[24]

In 1910, the year before Linda left Baggot Street, there were fifty one nurses employed in the hospital and from the time the course of training had started ten years before over ninety nurses had been trained. Of these forty four had joined private nursing homes or were working privately; six were on the staff of workhouse infirmaries; ten had married; five were matrons of hospitals; five were sisters in Baggot Street itself and three had died. Incidentally 1910 also saw the installation of an electric lift at a cost of £359.[25]

A number of references testify to Linda's ability as a nurse and to her sympathy for her patients. For example Robert Howard M.B., B.CH. Gynaecologist in Baggot Street wrote; 'Nurse Linda Kearns ... has proved herself to be a painstaking, intelligent nurse and has lost no opportunity of acquiring knowledge. I have pleasure in recommending Nurse L. Kearns as a well qualified nurse, kind and considerate to those placed under her care.' Another testimony written by Francis T Heuston M.D. FRCSI. praised her as 'a thoroughly trained nurse, who will perform any duties entrusted to her with ability, zeal and efficiency. Miss L. Kearns has a kind and sympathetic manner which is much appreciated by patients under her care'. Linda's parish priest of her home parish of Dromard, Rev. Patrick McNulty in his reference written in 1907, described her as 'a child of respected parents and belongs to a very old and respected family. She has been exceedingly well educated at home and for several years in Belgium and France. She has always been steady and industrious and she will be found trustworthy and faithful in the discharge of her duties'.[26] Fr. McNulty's mention of France in relation to Linda's education would seem to be inaccurate.

Although by all accounts Linda's time in Baggot Street Hospital was happy and successful, she did have at least one unpleasant encounter in the operating room. Apparently for some reason the surgeon 'aimed a kick at her' and she retaliated by throwing a blood-soaked swab at him, striking him 'between the two eyes'. Since now he was desterilized, he was forced to leave the room, change gear and return, a chastened man according to Linda.[27]

Linda left Baggot Street in December 1911, having tendered her resignation the previous October.[28] Shortly afterwards she was employed as a nurse attendant to Maurice Lindsey O'Connor Morris a substantial landowner of Gortnamona (formerly known as Mount Pleasant), Tullamore, Co. Offaly. Maurice was the only son of William O'Connor Morris, an Oxford graduate and county court judge for Roscommon. William was the author of a number of books including *Memories and Thoughts of a Life*. In the preface of this book he wrote: 'though always a Liberal, and a scion of a family true to the creed of Henry Grattan, I am a decided Unionist; but, while I believe that the unqualified maintenance of the Union is the only refuge Ireland can find from revolutionary anarchy, I am not blind to ills which the Union has –not caused—but brought in its train'.[29] His son Maurice Lindsey graduated in Arts from Trinity College, Dublin in 1887 and was shortly afterwards called to the Bar. A brilliant scholar, he was for a time private secretary to the Chancellor, Lord Ashbourne. He inherited Gortnamona in 1904. Although he was strong and robust in his youth and excelled on the cricket and football fields, he suffered a severe decline in health which left him an invalid requiring constant nursing care. However despite this he retained his fine sense of humour and kindly nature. In an effort to improve his health he sought out the benefits of a change of climate, spending time in France, Switzerland and Egypt. Linda, who had a high regard for him, accompanied him on his travels and in all they spent about four and half years out of the country.[30] A pair of amethyst drop earrings which he gave Linda as a present are now in the possession of her daughter. Maurice and Linda were back in Ireland by July 1914, when O'Connor Morris made his will in which he bequeathed Linda the sum of £2,500 'provided the said Linda Kearns is my nurse at the time of my death, that is that she is actually nursing me or is only away for a temporary holiday with my assent... All the rest, residue, and remainder of my property both real and personal I leave to my sisters...' He nominated his youngest sister Gertrude as his executrix.[31] It would appear that he and Linda went abroad again sometime after the drafting of the will and in all probability they were out of the country when Linda's mother, Catherine, died, aged sixty six on 10 March 1915. Her husband who survived her by six years erected a headstone to her memory in Dromard cemetery. Within two years of her mother's death, Linda's brother, Michael died. Two others who are buried in the same grave as Catherine, Thomas and Michael are Mary, the eldest of the family who died in 1942 and John Lucey who died in 1987.

    O'Connor Morris, who was unmarried and 'left no lawful children or other more remote lawful issue', died on Friday, 11 February, 1916, aged 50 in Gortnamona. The funeral service, at which Linda was listed as one of the chief mourners, was conducted by Rev J.T.Webster, rector of Ballyboy and Rev R.S. Craig, rector of Tullamore. The burial took place in Killoughey graveyard in the family plot.[32]

O'Connor Morris had investments in several companies mostly outside Britain and Ireland. Among the largest were £1000 in each of the following: The Argentine Great Western Railway, The Interoceanic Railway of Mexico and the Antofagasta Chile and Bolivia Railway. He had also invested heavily in The British Columbia Electric Railway and The Buenos Ayres and Pacific Railway. The total value of his shares at the time of his death was over £6,000.[33]

Two months after O'Connor Morris's death Linda was back in Dublin taking part in the Easter Rising.

Chapter Two
Active Service 1916-1920

Three particular experiences influenced Linda Kearns' decision to become involved in the revolutionary movement. The first was a visit she paid to the typhus hospital in Belmullet, Co. Mayo in 1911 or 1912. By this time she had finished her training in Baggot Street but had not yet gone abroad with O'Connor Morris. Her sister, whom she doesn't name in her account of this period, was already in Belmullet nursing the patients. Typhus was at epidemic proportions in Mayo at that time. 'I was horrified at the conditions prevailing in the hospital,' she writes in her memoir. 'It was not a hospital at all; it was only an old barn that was converted for this purpose. You could see the sky through the ceiling and walls and the patients were lying in filth on the floor. It occurred to me that it was time that the government responsible for that state of affairs should be expelled from the country.'[1]

The second significant influence on her thinking was Thomas McDonagh the 1916 leader, whom she met when he was a patient in Miss Quinn's, 27 Mountjoy Square. Linda was visiting a patient there when the meeting with McDonagh took place. She met him a couple of other times before the Rising and in the course of one their conversations she told him of her experience in Belmullet whereupon 'he preached an eloquent sermon to me about the misdeeds of the British Government in Ireland.'

The Gaelic League was also influential in Linda's life. She was very enthusiastic about learning Irish and attended private Irish classes 'somewhere in Baggot Street' before 1916.[2] She visited the Tourmakeady Gaeltacht in Mayo three summers in succession.[3]

On the Monday of Easter Week 1916, a neighbour, John O Mahony, the proprietor of Fleming's Hotel, 32 Gardiner Place visited Linda where she lived, a couple of doors away at no. 29 and asked her to set up a casualty centre for Volunteers who might be wounded in the fighting. He issued her with a pass on which was written 'Please admit Nurse Kearns.' It was signed by Éamon de Valera and it enabled her to enter the G.P.O. if required. She was of the opinion that she would be asked to act as a messenger between Boland's Mills and the G.P.O. In the event the only use she made of the pass was to bring a clean shirt to John O Mahony![4] O Mahoney, a native of Thomastown, Co. Kilkenny was heavily involved in the Sinn Féin and Volunteer movements. His hotel was a meeting place for prominent republicans and it was there Seán Mac Diarmada and Thomas Clarke stayed the night before the Rising. In the round up after the fighting he was sent to Frongoch, the internment camp in Wales.[5]

On the Wednesday of Easter Week Linda opened a hospital in an empty house belonging to a titled lady in North Great Georges Street. She put a Red Cross flag in one of the windows. Bandages, dressings and disinfectants were obtained from a chemist's shop called Toomeys. The Toomeys were strong republicans. Linda was assisted by six girls and two boys who were to operate as stretcher bearers. However the only casualties who arrived for treatment were two British soldiers who were suffering from hand wounds. One of them thought that he was in a British military hospital. The following morning Linda, under protest, closed the hospital on the orders of a British officer. He informed her that the wounded could be treated in the Mater and Jervis' Street hospitals. After that she walked around the streets seeking out wounded Volunteers who might need medical attention. On Friday, a man who was staying in O Mahony's hotel told her that he had seen the body of The O Rahilly lying in a lane off Moore's Street. Together they set off with a stretcher to rescue the body. They succeeded in getting through the barricade at the Parnell Street end of Moore's Street but a British officer who was standing by the body told them there was no point in removing him as he was quite dead.

Linda became involved again in the revolutionary movement when Michael Collins and Diarmaid O Hegarty called to see her early in 1917. They asked her to carry messages to a man named White who lived at Ballinabole about three miles from Collooney, Co. Sligo. White transferred the despatches to Alec McCabe who was on the run at the time. Afterwards she found out that these messages were connected with the I.R.B. On another occasion she carried a despatch to Kilroys at Newport, Co. Mayo. On yet another occasion she was sent to the fair in Ballinasloe with a letter for a man whose name she couldn't remember but who gave her a despatch to bring back to Diarmaid O Hegarty. Sometimes she brought back little bags of 'eggs' (small explosives)[6] to Dublin which were sent up from Sligo by Alec McCabe. These she delivered to Diarmaid O Hegarty at different locations. She was engaged in this type of activity for several years. In her memoir she says; 'I was able to carry on this work because to a certain extent I was my own boss. I had no regular employment. My sister and I kept a nurses' home in Gardiner Place. We did not normally take patients.' Linda and her sister Katie made an exception to this rule of keeping patients when Kathleen Clarke, wife of the executed 1916 leader Tom Clarke, became very seriously ill on her return to Ireland after her release from jail in England, (18 February 1919). Mrs. Clarke remained in 29 Gardiner Place for seven weeks where in her own words 'death and myself had a big tussle.' It is strange that neither she nor her sister Madge Daly mention Linda's name or the name of the nursing home in their accounts. Madame Markievicz who had been in Holloway prison with Kathleen Clarke came to visit her in the nursing home.[7]

Linda was never a member of Cumann na mBan but she did give lectures on First Aid for the Ranelagh branch which met at Cullenswood House and for the central branch in 25 Parnell Square. Molly Hyland and Miss Hoban were prominent in the Ranelagh branch while Kathleen Clarke, Mrs Ceannt and Miss O Rahilly were asssociated with the Central branch.

It would appear that Linda's work of carrying despatches and boxes of small explosives was mostly conducted between Sligo and Dublin. She worked closely with three of the principal Sligo leaders: Alec McCabe, Frank Carty and Billy Pilkington. She tells us that up to the time she bought her own car, all her journeys to and from the West were by train. On one such journey she came very close to be captured when she was bringing back a box of explosives to Dublin. 'I was carrying a box of eggs which had been given me at Teeling's monument, Collooney by a boy called Marron, a messenger from Alec McCabe. Our train was held up at Longford station by the Black and Tans. I was taken out and searched but I left the box of 'eggs' in the train. I returned to my carriage where I found the box untouched . The Black and Tans evidently never suspected that an egg box could contain anything but eggs. I think I delivered this to John O Mahony.'[8]

In 1920, Linda was the owner of a car, a Ford Touring model fitted with a hood. This may have been her second car. In 1918 she owned a car with a Mayo registration IZ 50.[9] She probably purchased this vehicle when she was on Achill island off the Mayo coast nursing victims of the flu epidemic. Interestingly, family sources insist that not one of her patients died and that she herself attributed her success to the use of poitín as medicine.[10] It is unclear whether her work on Achill in 1918 was done on a voluntary basis. She was known to have used part of the money she received from O'Connor Morris to purchase her first vehicle.[11] The fact that she had a car at her disposal meant that her role in the revolutionary movement changed. According to Vinnie Byrne, one of Michael Collins' squad, her driving ability was extremely useful in her intelligence work for Collins. Incidentally Vinnie said that although he knew of her and her activities he never met her. Linda came to the aid of another of Collins' squad, Frank Thornton, who in a bizarre incident, had accidentally wounded Tony Woods a Dublin I.R.A. officer. Her nursing skills were apparently put to good effect since Woods survived into old age.[12] In April, 1920 she drove Alec McCabe to Sligo from Dublin. McCabe who had spent ten days on hunger strike in Mountjoy Prison was released in a very weak condition and moved to St. Vincent's Hospital on 14 April. Fearing re-arrest when he left hospital he discharged himself.[13]

The details on Linda's application for a pension under the *Military Service Act, 1934*, afford important information on the extent of her involvement in the national struggle for the period 1916 –1923 which included the Easter Rising, the War of Independence and the Civil War. Her application was successful and she was accorded Grade D status which entitled her to a pension of £101/5/0 per annum. According to the service certificate she was actively involved for the duration of the Easter Rebellion but not at all for the year following i.e. up to 31 March, 1917. Her involvement from 1 April, 1917 to 31, March, 1918 was '$1/12$ of Entire Period'. This increased to '$1/6$ of Entire Period' for the following two years: 1 April, 1918 to 31, March, 1920. The following year, during which she was arrested and imprisoned, she was adjudged to have been '$2/3$ of Entire Period' on active service. Finally, from 1 April, 1921 to 30, September, 1923, except for six months after the signing of the Treaty, she was on active service for the 'Entire Period'. Her period of service was considerably enhanced by the fact that participation in the Easter Rising was counted as four years. According to the act the highest possible pension was £350 p.a. which a General Staff Officer on full service was entitled to. Under the heading *Forces in which Active Service was Rendered* of the certificate, Linda was deemed to have been a member of the Irish Volunteers up to March 1919 and from that date until September, 1923 of Óglaigh na hÉireann. It is interesting to note that the service certificate confirms that she was not a member of Cumann na mBan.[14] Her nephew Séamus Mulligan recalled that she was at pains to point out that she was never a member of this women's organisation.[15]

Linda's involvement in the national struggle entailed three particular roles; despatch carrying, the transport of arms and ammunition, and the tending of the wounded at ambush scenes. In later years she told one of her relatives that 'we did the dirty work, carrying despatches, putting ourselves in danger'.[16] According to Vinnie Byrne, she frequented an office in Phibsboro which was in the charge of Liam Tobin, Collins' principal officer and that her real importance lay in the fact that she had a car. Linda herself told her own daughter that Collins sometimes travelled with her. However she resented the fact that he would never apologise when he kept her waiting while he conducted one of his meetings. She disliked being taken for granted as she saw it.[17] Her residence, 29 Gardiner Place was one of Collins' safe houses. In her book, *Michael Collins and the Women in his Life*, Meda Ryan describes an incident concerning Collins in Linda's house which was related to her by Leslie Price, a former member of Cumann na mBan; 'He (Collins) was at dinner in Linda Kearns' nurses home one day when suddenly Auxiliaries burst in. Mick, plate and cutlery in hand, in a split second slid under the table. Shielded by the diners and tablecloth he crouched while the Auxies breezed past to look under beds, in cupboards, and corners. Mick and plate did not emerge until the last sound of the military had died and Linda gave the all clear.'[18]

In the autumn of 1920 Linda operated extensively in the Sligo area. She was told to make contact with Frank Carty at the Harp and Shamrock Hotel, The Mall, Sligo, which at that time was the principal meeting-place for republicans. If she found it impossible to communicate with the volunteers she brought her messages to Michael Nevin, the manager of Connolly's licensed premises and later the Mayor of Sligo. Nevin, according to Linda, was 'the keyman for despatches'.[19] He was intelligence officer of the Sligo Company of the I.R.A. and later was appointed Brigade I.O. He says in his own account; 'I never succeeded in making contact with the R.I.C. or British forces in Sligo. My principal source of information was through Fr. J.J. Hanley of the college staff, also chaplain to the Volunteers. He was a personal friend of District Inspector Russell who came to Sligo on transfer from Ballymote'.[20]

Linda worked closely with Carty's brigade. She says in her account- 'Both Frank and Billy Pilkington seemed to be in command of that brigade. I had a good deal to do with Billy. I was used now chiefly for carrying guns before and after an engagement. It seemed as if a couple of flying columns were using the same material. I would bring them to Chaffpool one day and perhaps the next day back to Grange'.[21]

According to District Inspector Russell of Sligo, Linda spent about six weeks in her sister Annie's house in Lisconny, near Collooney prior to her capture on 20 November, 1920.[22] In fact she was somewhat longer in the area since the ambush took place on Thursday, 30 September. This carefully planned attack between Buninadden and Tubbercurry resulted in the death of twenty-two year old District Inspector Brady. Two other R.I.C. men were wounded, one seriously. According to the police report: 'D.I. Brady, Head Constable O'Hara and seven men from Tubbercurry went from Sligo on duty via motor lorry. They left Sligo for their station about 4p.m. taking a different route via Ballymote. When they arrived at Leitrim, about 2 miles from Tubbercurry on the road between Buninadden and Tubbercurry they were fired on with rifles from an elaborately prepared ambush behind loopholed walls situated on elevated ground on each side of the road . The spot was a regular death trap and afforded no chance of success to the police, even if they had been in a position to dismount and attack'.

Brady sustained three wounds in the region of the kidneys which the police maintained were caused by dumdum or expanding bullets. The calf of Head Constable O'Hara's right leg was 'practically blown away'. Constable Brown was slightly injured. The lorry continued on under heavy fire to Tubbercurry where it was discovered that the telephone wires had been cut. A number of police set out for Sligo by lorry to report on the event as a result of which District Inspectors Russell and Dease, accompanied by sixteen police and ten soldiers under the command of an army officer drove to Tubbercurry, arriving there at 11p.m. They found that D.I. Brady had died at about 8.30 p.m. 'His naked body was lying on the kitchen floor having been washed after death. H.C. O'Hara was lying in a room off the kitchen suffering intense pain. On seeing this the R.I.C and military left the station and carried out reprisals against property in Tubbercurry which their officers were unable to prevent.'

When news of the ambush reached the town, some of the people, fearing the worst, shuttered their windows. Others left their homes and took refuge in the convent and workhouse. One shopkeeper, whose large premises was completely destroyed, spent the night in a quarry. The police and military began the destruction shortly after midnight. Shots were fired indiscriminately and many properties, particularly in the square, were destroyed. Around 2.30am a party of the military headed for the creamery at Ballyara and burned it to the ground. The manager T.H. Murricane hearing the explosions in Tubbercurry removed the accounts books and other records. His wife was lucky to escape with her life. Achonry creamery came under attack twice in the early hours of the 21st. On the first occasion at about 2.30am little damage was done. However the military returned at 4.30am and set fire to the building. The retail store was destroyed but the manager P.J. Condon and about thirty helpers succeeded in saving most of the machinery.

On the night following the destruction reprisals were expected again when word went around that Constable O'Hara's life was in danger. In the event he was removed to Dr. Steevens' Hospital in Dublin where he recovered. On Saturday, 2 October the inquest on District Inspector Brady had to be abandoned by the coroner Dr. O'Hart when only seven jurors turned up. The body was brought from Ballymote to Dublin by train. After requiem mass in Aughrim Street church he was buried in Glasnevin cemetery. John Joseph Brady was twenty two at the time of his death. He was son of Captain Louis Brady, the Harbour Master at Dublin and nephew of P.J. Brady M.P.

A week after the ambush, Tubbercurry was still fearful. Some people had affixed crucifixes to their front doors and 'little knots of people were standing at several corners, others in close proximity to the ruined buildings; all were discussing from various standpoints what had happened. The purr of the engine of an approaching motor car called everyone to immediate attention. Heads were thrust through doorways. The noise of a motor car seemed to convey an ominous meaning for the people, and whether friend or foe the occupants of a motor car were the objects of a careful scrutiny… With these people it was no longer an effort of the imagination to arrive at the meaning of reprisals. They had tasted of the bitterness of which they had only read and heard of before… Adjoining the chapel was a heap of stone and mortar in an empty space where a house once stood. The warped bars of a charred bedstead peeping up from the heap of ruins told its tale'.[23]

Linda was on standby in case of injuries to any of the volunteers at the Moneygold ambush between Grange and Cliffoney on 25 October 1920 the same day that Terence MacSwiney the Lord Mayor of Cork died in Brixton prison after seventy four days on hunger strike. Thirty eight I.R.A. men were involved in Moneygold, some in the firing group with others acting as look-outs. Among those who took part were: Seamus Devins, Brigadier, Grange, Billy Pilkington, Commandant, Sligo, Eugene Gilbride, Captain, Grange, Andy Conway, Captain, Cliffoney, Paddy Branley, Captain, Glencar, Ned Bofin, Captain, Rosses Point and Willie Devins, Quarter Master, Grange.

The site for the ambush was carefully chosen by Seamus Devins and Billy Pilkington at the hill known as Druim a Cruisha. Trenches were dug and the Cliffoney R.I.C. were lured out on patrol in the following manner.

The I.R.A cut of the shafts of a cart belonging to a man whose sympathies were pro-British. He duly reported the incident to the police who would be expected to investigate. However some of them, sensing a trap, were reluctant to leave the barracks. They also knew that since Cliffoney was the only police station on the road between Sligo and Bundoran, it was quite likely that they would come under attack sooner or later. However, on being reminded by the sergeant Patrick Perry, that as members of His Majesty's forces it was their duty to look into the matter, they set out on their bicycles at 11a.m. Nine officers comprised the patrol: Sergeant Perry, and Constables Patrick Laffey, Patrick Keown, Patrick Lynch, Clarke, Michael Rourke, Spratt, John McCormack and Patrick Joyce. Sergeant James Casey remained on in the barracks.

The masked I.R.A. men had taken up positions on both sides of the road. When the R.I.C. came into sight they were called on to surrender but instead reached for their weapons. The engagement lasted about five minutes and when it was over Perry, Laffey, and Keown lay dead. Lynch was critically wounded. Clarke and O'Rourke also sustained injuries and they were removed to a Dublin hospital. Spratt and Joyce were uninjured. The attackers, after capturing the arms and ammunition, left the scene in different directions. They had suffered no casualties. Linda stayed on for some time to tend to the wounded, thus leaving herself open to possible identification at a later date. A small bowl and pieces of bandages were found at the roadside near what appeared to be a bloodstain.

An eyewitness gave the following account of the ambush and its aftermath:

'I was working in the field quite close to the place. I did not notice the police going past but I suddenly heard the report of shots. The firing was as fast as it was sudden and I would say that it lasted about five minutes. I did not go near the place for awhile—for although the firing ceased I was not sure if it was safe. When I did go I saw the priest coming towards the spot. The first man I saw lying on the road was

Constable Clarke. I thought he was dead but later on I saw that he was one of the wounded. About three or four yards from him I saw Sergeant Perry lying face downwards. He was dead at the time. Constable Laffey was beside him lying on his right side and he was dead also. Constable Keown was some distance away, lying close to his bicycle. He was also dead. Constable Lynch was in near the bank. His head appeared to be resting on a stone. He had his right hand on his breast and his fingers were twitching as if in pain. Mrs Lynch (Constable Lynch's wife) was beside him at the time. I spoke to him but he only opened his eyes; he did not answer. Fr. Crehan (of Grange) and Dr. Martin (of Cliffoney) were there at the time and were attending the men. The scene was terrible. There was nothing but pools of blood and caps and bicycles thrown around'.

The bodies of the dead were taken back to Cliffoney and the wounded were removed to the County Infirmary. Constable Patrick Lynch, aged 33 and married with two children, died that evening. His remains were brought back to Bailieboro, Co. Cavan. Constable Patrick Keown's body was taken to Belleek, Co. Fermanagh. He was 25 and single. Two lorries conveyed the remains of Sergeant Perry and Constable Patrick Laffey from Cliffoney to Sligo. On the front of the first one there hung a large banner on which was written: 'Sinn Fein Victory—Three Widows and 17 children'. Perry aged 51, a native of Ballivor, Co. Meath left a wife and ten children and was buried near Boyle. Laffey, 41 was married with five children. He was a native of Woodlawn, Co.Galway where he was buried.

According to *The Sligo Champion*: 'Since the occurrence, the people of the localities of Grange and Cliffoney and even in the surrounding districts have lived in a state of absolute terror. Few people have trusted the shelter for any single night. From Monday night the auxiliary forces have been operating and practically every house has been searched.' Seamus Devins' house was burned to the ground as was his hay and turf. His mother who was in the house fled in terror. Eugene Gilbride's house was also searched but not set on fire. Grange fair on the following Thursday was interrupted and the people were given ten minutes to vacate the village. When the reign of terror was over several houses lay in ruins including Currid's, Higgins' Harkins' and Conway's. The house of Grange schoolteacher Tom Burke was broken into but not burned. Fr. Flanagan Hall, Cliffoney, a fine two-storey building was one of the first to come under attack. Afterwards the words *'vacated home of the murder gang'* were painted on the ruin. Ballintrillick creamery was also severely damaged. According to *The Roscommon Herald*:

...'the burning of Grange Temperance Hall was by far the most serious by reason of its proximity to the chapel. The hall which was a magnificent building with beautifully stained glass windows and divided from the chapel by a small path about five feet wide is now almost a complete ruin. The doors front and back were broken in by large stones. The billiard table inside was badly damaged and all around the entire hall was saturated with petrol. Particular attention must have been paid to the library as this portion of the building was completely gutted, not a trace remaining of the shelves, bookcases and presses and over a thousand volumes of expensive books'.

After the raiders had departed, the local priest Fr. Crehan rushed into the chapel and removed the vestments and sacred vessels. He paid tribute to all the people both Protestants and Catholics who had sought to save the hall. This wholesale burning and destruction of peoples' homes made a profound impression on Linda and she mentioned it on a number of occasions during her fund raising tour of the United States a couple of years later. Reprisals were expected in Sligo town but in the event did not materialise. However in the words of *The Sligo Champion*:

'the Sinn Féin flag which was in mourning for the Lord Mayor of Cork, hoisted from the Municipal buildings, was taken down on Wednesday morning. The flag and window blinds of the tri-colour, together with pictures and documents appertaining to the Club were taken down from the Sinn Féin Hall in Albert Street. The Sinn Féin flag over the infirmary was also taken down, but these were the only occurrences in the town'.[24]

A couple of months after the Moneygold ambush a twenty three year old married man from the locality made two statements to the R.I.C. in Sligo. In the first he gave the names of a number of I.R.A. suspects whom he said he had seen on the evening of the engagement. In the second he described his own kidnapping by members of the volunteers who decided not to shoot him but warned him to leave the country. In his report dated 30 January 1921 District Inspector Russell said that this man had:

'... called at my office and stated that on 23inst he was threatened by volunteers. I took a statement from him which he signed. From previous knowledge which myself and the C.I. had regarding facts he knew concerning the Cliffoney murders and were in fact expecting him to call at the barrack. I sent at once for the C.I. The latter questioned him very closely and drew from him a statement showing that he was a most important witness against several of the murderers. On his own invitation he was taken on charge as a Crown witness'.

Chief Inspector Neylon wrote that the informer 'has been in police uniform since he was taken into Sligo R.I.C. Barrack and is known as 'Constable Richard Black'. Neylon recommended that 'Black' be retained as a crown witness and that it was imperative he be well guarded. The police had a suspicion that Frank Carty and Joe McDevitt had taken part in the ambush; a suspicion which was based on the evidence of one of the survivors, Sergeant Joyce and also on the following description based on 'Black's' account: 'one of the men whose name he did not know carried a rifle. He was a tall stout man, dark overcoat, clean shaven, had a peculiar walk of which he gave a demonstration. Another of the men struck him as being remarkable. He was a very short stout man with very curly hair, clean shaven, very round head and face and carried a rifle'. At this time both Carty and McDevitt were in prison and the R.I.C. were obviously keen to build up a damning case against them. Incidentally neither Billy Pilkington nor Linda were named by the informer.

'Black' told the police he had been kidnapped close to his father's house by between thirty and forty men on the night of 23 January. 'They were all partly masked, some of them had only mufflers around their necks and mouths. Ned Moffat, Gortnaleck and John Gallagher, Grange shouted 'hands up'. Michael Oates, Dominick Feeney and Dominick J. Feeney ordered me face the wall. James Shelton ordered me do the same. Ned Moffat said "Face it you cur, it's not the rotten Government you are dealing with now. If you don't face it I'll make you do it with a bullet".' His hands were tied with a hempen rope and he was then marched some distance 'towards Glengarragh bog'. Some of the party were in favour of shooting him declaring him to be 'long enough a government spy'. He was told he would be given a bullet 'the same as we put through Perry's mouth at Brierty's Cross'. However the decision was taken not to shoot him but he was warned 'to leave the Irish coast by Saturday'. Black supplied the police with the names of twenty volunteers involved in the kidnapping. A couple of days after giving his statements in Sligo 'Constable Black' was moved to the R.I.C. camp in Gormanstown and later to Dublin. He apparently fell into bad health but in July he was deemed well enough to be brought to Mountjoy Prison for the purpose of identifying Frank Carty who was incarcerated there at that time. Neylon informed Dublin Castle that 'Black' could be vital in gaining a conviction in Carty's murder trial which was pending. In his opinion 'Black' should be given 'the opportunity of seeing Frank Carty and asked if he can identify him as one of the party of armed men whom he saw coming from the scene of the murders on evening of 26/10/20. In his statement he described Carty very accurately; appearance, figure, peculiar gait, and he said he would know him if he saw him again'. However 'Black' himself seemed less enthusiastic in a letter he wrote on 11 July, 1921: 'I was kidnapped some time about February this year by armed and masked men, taken to Ben Bulben mountain where after a short confinement I was released. I became very ill with the fright I got and since then I have forgotten all about what actually happened in last October'.

Three days later, accompanied by Head Constable James Fleming, he was brought to Mountjoy. The identification did not take place however because according to Fleming: 'Just as the Deputy Governor was going out for Carty, who was at exercise at the time, he met two warders bringing in the prisoner who was after spraining his ankle. The medical officer stated that Carty would not be able to stand on his foot for at least one week'. For some reason Dublin Castle decided that 'no further action should be taken at present'.

'Constable Black' named twenty men whom he said were involved in his kidnapping. In the official report they were all described as being of 'bad character and of local importance.' They were: Edward Moffat, Gortnaleck, Grange, aged 22, a farmer; Peter Gilmartin, Gortnaleck, Grange, 21, a farmer; Dominick Feeney, Cashelgarron, 27, farmer; Dominick J.Feeney, Cashelgarron, 28, farmer; Michael Oates, Cashelgarron, 30, farmer; Thomas Gorevan, Cashelgarron, 24, farmer; James Shelton, Cashelgarron, 34, farmer; Charles Haran, Cashelgarron, 30, blacksmith; John Haran, Cashelgarron 26, farmer; John Gallagher, Grange, 23, labourer; Thomas Leonard, Grange, 23, farmer; John McGowan, Barnaderrig, labourer (age not given); Francis Feeney, Barnaderrig, 52, farmer; Eugene Brady, Ardnaglass, 20, farmer; Patrick Currid, Barnaderrig, 19, farmer; Cormac Feeney, Grogath, 22 farmer; John Friel, Cashelgarron, 26, farmer; John Leydon,

Kilcat, 30, labourer; Daniel Kilfeather, Kiltykere, 23, farmer; Patrick Farrell, Cashelgarron, 40, farmer.

According to the report signed by District Inspector Russell, Edward Moffat, Peter Gilmartin, Dominick Feeney, Michael Oates and Thomas Gorevan 'were arrested on 30th ult. on another charge and are at present in Sligo gaol. The others have not been arrested pending orders'.[25]

Chapter Three
Capture

'Every detail of my arrest is vividly implanted in my memory- never to fade from it. The brain sometimes receives certain impressions so deeply that they are, as it were seared into our very mind, and so remain, never to grow fainter, or to become dimmed as the years pass.' So wrote Linda in her book *In Times of Peril*.[1] In her statement written later for the Military Archive, she gives a more detailed version of her capture in Sligo on the night of 20 November 1920. On that date she was driving her car which had as occupants, Seamus Devins, Eugene Gilbride and Andy Conway, towards Ballisodare when a mixed party of police and military stopped the vehicle and discovered a substantial quantity of arms and ammunition.[2]

Linda's account of the circumstances leading up to the arrest is somewhat at variance with those of Eugene Gilbride[3] and Tom Scanlon,[4] both of whom say that Linda did not take the pre-arranged route to Ballisodare to ensure a safe exit out of Sligo. However, in her defence, it is important to emphasis that Devins as commanding officer would have the final say in the choosing of the route.

'I got a message from Marron', she says in her account, ' to report with my car at 7p.m. at the Harp and Shamrock, Sligo and there await further instructions. I went there and waited and a boy came in with a despatch which he showed me. He was to accompany Nurse Kearns to a certain crossroads on the road to Lough Gill.' On the way they stopped at a house where a man, whom she doesn't name, placed two guns in the car. When they reached the cross-roads, the name of which, Linda couldn't remember, Devins, Gilbride and Conway were already there. She was told that they were expecting another car to take them to Frenchpark for an attack on the Auxiliary headquarters there. Linda's role was her usual one: to bring the arms to where the engagement was to take place. When the second car failed to turn up Devins decided that Linda would transport himself and the two others as well as the arms in her car.

'Jim Devins then took me down a little way along the road by the shore of Lough Gill and he said to me : "Have you taken the oath?" I said: "No". "You had better take it now, not that it will make any difference. If you wanted to give us away you could have done so long ago. But those are my orders." I repeated the oath after him. It was a thrilling and unforgettable moment in the dark of the night by the side of the road.'[5]

Linda was probably mistaken in regard to the location of the meeting place with the three I.R.A. men. Eugene Gilbride is more definite in his information when he says that the meeting took place in Glencar 'at the end of Paddy Branley's land.'[6] The lake was probably Glencar and not Lough Gill.

They drove back to Sligo and according to Linda a lad called Feeney guided them through the back streets out of the town and 'he had barely jumped off the car when we ran straight into a lorry load of Auxiliaries.' Eugene Gilbride gives a more detailed account:

'She was to bring the car by Wine St., Adelaide St. and pick up Harry Brehony at Summerhill College and from there bring the car to Belladrohid Bridge, Ballisodare by a back road. Linda was told the way to go and she said: 'Are we afraid of anyone? We will go this way, it's straighter.' She went by No.1 and No.2 barracks. When we got outside the town we knew she should have gone to the college.'[7]

Tom Scanlon is quite scathing of Linda in his version of events:

'They were to go through the town (Sligo) and we had scouts along the way to meet them. Linda Kearns didn't want this and she went straight through the town... We had taken all the necessary precautions. Even in Sligo we were to take a side route. She seemed to think that this arrangement was a waste of time and she insisted, against the instructions of the scout who was with her, that she would go by another route and she did. So when they were outside the town at the borough boundary the scout said 'I had better get out here.' This was the lad they had brought to the college. They stopped the car and he had only gone about five or ten yards when he heard an order 'Put your hands up.'[8]

Linda thought that there was a gap through which she could drive at speed past the lorry but Devins told her not to attempt it. When she stopped the car he drew his revolver but she put it down with her hand. There then followed scenes of absolute mayhem. The soldiers, who according to Linda, were wild with drink began to fire shots at random. This capture was their second big coup of the night for unknown to Linda and her companions another car had been halted at Union Wood, a short time previously and the five occupants were already on the lorry. They were: Dr. Peter Conlon of Geevagh, Joe McDevitt of Dublin, Martin Flynn of the Co. Council clerical staff, Thomas Cawley, Pound Street and John Farrell, Mail Coach Road, Sligo, the driver of the car.[9]

Devins, Gilbride and Conway were struck with rifles and revolvers. According to Gilbride 'Jimmy Devins got the worst. He was bleeding mad.' Gilbride himself was knocked unconscious and came to after he was carried to the lorry. Linda was put back into her car with two auxiliaries and told to drive back to Sligo. The beating started again when they arrived in the barracks and intensified when the police recognized some of the rifles as ones captured after the Moneygold ambush.[10] The occupants of the first car were also beaten. In *In Times of Peril* Linda writes; 'I saw Dr. Conlon at one side of the room and a Black and Tan holding a revolver over his head and insisting that the doctor endorse a cheque which he had in his possession so that the Black and Tan could cash it. I also saw Professor McDevitt being beaten and all his things taken from his pockets.' Linda's own leather overcoat, gloves, wristlet watch and signet ring were forcibly taken from her and not returned.[11]

As the violence continued in the dayroom where in Gilbride's words they got 'a good hammering', Devins and Conway managed to exchange a few words with Linda regarding the line of defence she would take, reminding her that, according to a new order, anyone found with a gun could be shot on sight. Linda replied that she would say that everything in the car, including the guns and ammunition was hers and that she had given three men a lift after they had hailed her. 'I thought they would not shoot a woman. I stuck to this story to the end and I think it saved their lives.'[12]

After some time, Linda was searched by the Head Constable's daughter and she was removed to a lock-up; a tiny room with a hard bench and a stone floor. The night was bitterly cold. She then endured what she described as a night of horror. One of the prisoners was brought past her door and several shots were fired. Voices shouted; 'Will we shoot the girl next or do for one of the other fellows first?' She quickly realized that they were attempting to terrify her into making a confession. The questioning continued throughout the night. She was repeatedly asked where she was going when arrested. Her explanation was that she was to meet up with certain men but these were not the men arrested. At one point a military officer wearing an overcoat over his pyjamas came into the room to take up the questioning. He adopted a very conciliatory tone advising her that if she revealed the purpose of her journey and whom she was to meet she would be let go and the episode forgotten. He added that she was 'damned unlucky to have got herself into such a stew.' She gave him no information. After he left Linda received her worst beating of the night at the hands of an R.I.C. officer nicknamed 'Spud' Murphy. He struck her about the head, chest and mouth resulting in the dislocation of one of her front teeth. One of the Black and Tans, a Cockney, who was present, intervened on her behalf saying: 'Leave her halone, she might be as hinnocent as the child hunborn.'[13]

After the arrests the scout who had left Linda's car returned to Sligo and reported what had happened. According to Tom Scanlon the military had surrounded the barracks after Linda and her group had been brought in. Tom and other I.R.A. men 'lay for a few hours near the Market Cross and the next day, in the morning we sent in a doctor.'[14]

Later British soldiers painted the walls of the courthouse with notices such as *Up Cromwell, Up Lloyd George, To Hell with the Pope* and *Remember Balbriggan*. The latter notice referred to the attack of the Black and Tans on this Co. Dublin town a few weeks before. Sketches of coffins were also drawn on the courthouse, on houses in Chapel Street and on the shutters of several shops.[15]

On Sunday 21 November, the day after the capture, the house that Linda shared in Dublin with her sister Kate O'Connell and Kate's husband Jack, 29 Gardiner's Place was raided by the military. Kate was told that Linda had been arrested and was interrogated herself. In a letter to *The Sligo Champion* she described what happened:

> 'When the military raided my home and my private boudoir was burst open they were surprised to find that I was the only occupant and an invalid. The considerable damage done to my home was uncalled for considering that I offered my keys. The bill sent in by my plumber and locksmith amounts to over £12 for which amount I am sending an account to Dublin Castle. Neither my sister Linda Kearns nor I belong to any organisation outside the nursing world and I always maintain my house on non-sectarian and non-political lines.'

Kate said that Linda had been in the west of Ireland to negotiate the sale of a farm.[16]

On Monday night, 22 November, from about 9pm military from outside the town took possession of the streets of Sligo. Soldiers entered the Hibernian and Foresters' halls and everybody present in both halls were forced to put up their hands as they were searched. People were stopped and made account for their movements. *The Sligo Champion* reported that:

> 'even the most inoffensive citizens were treated roughly... the rough treatment was not confined to any section or class, it was indiscriminate and we have been given the names of several Protestant gentlemen who were assaulted. Despite anything that may have happened in the county, there has never been any friction between police and people here. This area is, we understand, under the control of the local police and military. But their functions were usurped on Monday night and the town was taken possession of by these men who had just come in, in the afternoon and for a few hours it was like hell let loose on an inoffensive populace. There was no interference with these men and their conduct towards inoffensive people was to put it mildly, unpardonable.'

There were allegations also that these 'visiting' military entered several houses and took money and valuables.[17]

This rampage of the military was probably influenced by the Bloody Sunday killings in Dublin (21 November) when fourteen suspected secret service agents were shot dead by the I.R.A. on the orders of Michael Collins. The police in Sligo believed (wrongly) that Linda, in the words of Chief Inspector Neylon, 'at the time of her arrest was conveying three County Sligo murderers to Dublin with stores of arms and ammunition to murder Crown Forces.'[18]

On Tuesday morning, 23 November, at 7pm while it was still dark, five lorries of military arrived in Dromard Linda's home area in Co. Sligo. The house of Matty and Thomas Clarke, Linda's first cousins was thoroughly searched but nothing incriminating was found. A new house built by Matt Clarke, but as yet unoccupied was broken into and the windows smashed. The military painted the walls with slogans such as; *Up Cromwell, Up LLoyd George* and *Beware Sinn Feiners*. The lorries then moved on to the Kilpatrick house which was also ransacked and the haggard was set on fire, completely destroying the contents of hay and corn. The Cliffoney area was also subjected to raids.[19]

Chief Inspector Neylon, in his official report to Dublin Castle, claimed that the arrests resulted from information which District Inspector Russell had received the previous day ...

> 'that on the night following at 11.30p.m. a quantity of rifles, revolvers and ammunition used and captured in connection with the Cliffoney ambush would leave Sligo by the Colloney road by motor. He reported the matter to me at 9a.m. on 20th inst. And we arranged the following plan of action. The matter to be kept a dead secret and no display of police activity to be made in the town; to requisition a military party to assist the police; to send a strong police and military patrol to a place some ten miles from Sligo and in a direction different to that in which the motors conveying the arms were to travel. Two lorries of police and two lorries of soldiers left Sligo at 9.30p.m. with H.C. Murphy in charge of the police who got special instructions how to act. On arrival at their supposed destination some bogus searches of houses were made. The party then returned towards Sligo by a circuitous route to the Collooney road, the police leading.'

He went on to give details of the arrest of the occupants of both cars. Neylon said Linda was about 5' 8' in height, (she was in fact two inches taller), of slight build, that she had a long thin face, long nose, a pale sallow complexion and protruding front teeth which were 'much exposed when speaking.' She wore glasses and he estimated her age at 40, which was considerably wide of the mark. He described her as 'cool and brazen.'[20]

The subsequent police investigation into the events leading up to Linda's arrest, as reported by District Inspector Russell, established that she had stayed with her sister Mrs Annie Mulligan at Lisconny, Collooney, Co. Sligo for about six weeks prior to 20 November. On that date she drove into Sligo between 1pm and 2pm and returned to Lisconny at 7pm that same evening. She left again around 8pm saying she was going to a dance in Beltra but instead she went back to Sligo. She had told the police when interrogated that she had returned to the Harp and Shamrock Hotel to recover a purse which she had found to be missing later. According to the proprietor of the hotel no one had called to look for a missing purse but that a woman answering Linda's description was in the hotel earlier in the day. The final part of Russell's report is interesting in that it throws light on the extent of police intelligence in the Sligo area at that time- 'From information in my possession she went to Glencar, 8 miles from Sligo, picked those men and arms there and was passing through the town at an hour it was expected no one would be met with. Her car had good lights because an unlighted car would be very suspicious.' Chief Inspector Neylon in his report wrote: 'I have private information from well-informed quarters that, for a long time prior to her arrest, Nurse Kearns was giving very active assistance to the I.R.A. carrying arms and despatches, and doing organizing work generally.'[21]

One of the items found in Linda's car was a flashlamp which she had given as a present to her six-year old nephew Séamus Mulligan the day before the arrest. She told Séamus she was going to a dance and that she needed the lamp in case anything went wrong with the car.[22]

Chapter Four

Imprisonment

The day after the arrest Linda and the other prisoners were moved from the barracks in Teeling Street to the nearby jail in Cranmore, the first of five prisons in which she would spend time over the next year or so. Here, while she was waiting for a wardress to bring her to her cell, she was subjected to verbal abuse from a policeman who also amused himself 'by taking accurate aim at my head with his rifle.' She feared she would become another victim 'shot while trying to escape.' Sligo Jail was dull, grey and cold. The following Wednesday she was awoken at 5am and told to prepare to move out of the prison. When she was taken to the gate she was astonished to see her car. Devins, Gilbride and the others who had been arrested the previous Saturday night were put on a lorry while Linda herself was ordered into her own car and driven along a route which she knew very well. Her driver wasn't particularly competent, at one point having taken the wrong turn found himself on a side road. He needed the assistance of one of the soldiers from the lorry to get him back on the main road again. The destination was Raughley where a British gunboat awaited their arrival. Dawn broke and the weather was fine: 'a perfect day, cold, crisp and clear. It was just heavenly to inhale the pure breezes and to hear the swish of the waves on the deck after my confined quarters.'[1]

Linda was very appreciative of the treatment she received on the gunboat. One officer in particular was especially kind to her, providing her with hot water, soap and a large soft towel. She hadn't had a proper wash in the time she was in custody in Sligo. This officer also procured a mirror, brush and comb for her and gave her his own nail file. Years later this act of kindness was still vivid in her mind.

The destroyer sailed to a point off Buncrana and late in the evening the prisoners were taken off and placed in a small boat to be brought ashore. Linda was terribly cold in the open boat and badly missed her coat and gloves. Dr. Conlon gave her his own overcoat and the other prisoners did their best to shield her from the wind. On arrival at the pier in Buncrana they were brought by lorry to Derry. They were made to squat on the floor of the vehicle, which was extremely uncomfortable. Linda and Joe McDevitt sat back to back to give each other support.

The prisoners spent four days in Derry Jail. The governor was reluctant to admit Linda because the jail was for men only. She was given accommodation in the hospital quarters which had no patients at the time. The warder, an old man, who was assigned to look after her, supplied an iron and she was able to wash and iron her clothes. A friend of Linda's who was a nurse living in Derry sent in her meals from a restaurant. Linda does not name this woman in her account. All in all, the time spent in Derry was quite pleasant.

The next stop for the Sligo prisoners was Belfast to which they were taken by an early train from Derry. The men were handcuffed to each other in pairs and Linda was handcuffed to a young officer. She was accompanied also by two wardresses. The twenty soldiers or so who made up the escort were quite cheerful and they joined in a sing-song with the prisoners. Cigarettes were exchanged and there was no objection when some of the men hid cigarettes in the turn-ups of their trousers and matches in their hair in anticipation of a further term in jail. On arrival at Belfast Jail Linda and her escort were refused admittance. The governor shut the door and the officer to whom Linda was handcuffed turned to her and said, 'What shall I do with you?', to which she replied, 'Let me go home.' 'I wish to God I could', he said. Her next stop was Victoria Barracks. Everyone seemed at a loss to know what to do with her and she found it amusing to watch the expression on the faces of the officers as each in turn tried to hand her on to someone else. By now it was late in the evening and Linda hadn't eaten anything since 5am- she had received a cup of cocoa before leaving Derry. A policeman brought her in some food that she paid for herself. After some time the two wardresses who had accompanied her from Derry arrived and she was put on a lorry, this time with police only. The lorry headed for the railway station and she was put on board a train bound for Armagh. By now she knew that she was being sent to the female prison there. There was a short delay at Armagh railway station as transport to the prison was awaited. Linda was held in the waiting room with three other women who were non-political prisoners. One of them offered her a pinch of snuff.

It was 8pm by the time she was finally within the walls of Armagh Jail. In *In Times of Peril* she writes: 'I reached the reception room and someone gave me a seat, and I heard a voice say kindly: "Are you very tired?" It was the first note of sympathy I had heard for many a long hour, and of course it completely broke down my self-control. I just laid my head on the table and cried –and cried.'[2]

Linda spent over four months on remand in Armagh Jail. During that time she failed to gain parole for Christmas 1920 and an attempt later to spring her was unsuccessful. On 11 March 1921 together with Seamus Devins, Eugene Gilbride and Andy Conway she was courtmartialled. Shortly after the courtmartial her father Thomas died at home in Sligo.

A fellow-prisoner in Armagh, Eily McAdam, wrote of Linda: 'I had heard much of her– who hadn't? I expected someone formidable. I found a loveable girl...... She could be grave too with a wise view of life; but mostly I remember her as a point of brightness in a dismal place.' Eily recalled an incident with the prison doctor who was intensely disliked by the prisoners. Apparently when they first met Linda greeted him with 'good morning doctor'! 'I am not accustomed to "good mornings" from prisoners', he replied. After making some complaint and ignoring his rudeness Linda said 'thank you doctor, that is if you are accustomed to "thank yous" from prisoners.' According to

Eily he was left speechless and the women were highly amused.[3]

Linda had a high regard for the governor, whom she described as 'a very competent and humane woman.' She told Linda on her arrival in the jail that as far as she was concerned the law of 'innocent until proven guilty' applied. She stressed however that it was her duty to prevent any attempt to escape and she asked Linda to give her word of honour that she would not entertain such a notion. When Linda refused she showed no anger. The governor insisted on high standards in her jail. 'The food was well cooked and cleanly served, the discipline was excellent and her subordinates were all most anxious to please their governor in every way. I was allowed an ordinary bed and ordinary washing basin, while in Mountjoy the women awaiting trial there had to sleep on plank beds.' Linda ordered that her dinner be sent in every day from the Beresford Arms Hotel. She does not explain how payment was made for these meals. Among Linda's visitors was Fr. McKeown of Carrickmacross whom she had previously met when on a pilgrimage to Lough Derg. Another caller was a district nurse who had to discontinue her visits when her local committee reported her.[4]

She kept in contact with her family and in a letter to *The Sligo Champion* dated 4 December 1920 her sister Kate wrote to inform the public of her whereabouts. In view of the fact that it was well known that Linda was in Armagh prison it is surprising to find that Lt.-Commander J.M. Kenworthy M.P. sought information from the Chief Secretary, Sir Hamar Greenwood as to her whereabouts in a letter dated 14 January 1921. He wrote that he 'had an enquiry from a relative of this lady who is most anxious to know.'[5] Kenworthy was an outspoken critic of British military policy in Ireland. Some of his colleagues considered him a traitor.

Linda, Eugene Gilbride, Andy Conway and Seamus Devins were courtmartialled at Victoria Barracks, Belfast on 11 March, 1921. The taking of evidence took place about three weeks earlier, also in Belfast. They were charged with the unlawful possession of 10 rifles, 1 automatic pistol, 1 revolver, 426 rifle cartridges, 2 rifle cartridges with flat noses and 13 pistol and revolver cartridges. Some of these weapons were identified as the property of the police involved in the Moneygold ambush. The following items were also found in Linda's car: field dressings, material for bandages, two masks, an oil bottle of a military or police pattern and a flashlamp. Another flashlamp was found in Devins' pocket. Devins also had on his person 'an ink sketch of a road leading from Skreen Creamery via Beltra to Carrignagat and Collooney.' This information is contained in the charge sheet and summary of evidence, dated 5 March 1921.[6]

Linda was brought by train to Belfast for this taking of evidence. For security reasons she was not allowed to sit in a corner seat but she did insist on being accompanied by a female attendant in accordance with escort regulations. She was kept overnight in the Bridewell. A meal was sent in which she paid for and she also ordered breakfast for the following morning. At the hearing the next day 'we amused ourselves by wondering what new version of the night of our arrest we would hear now. Well they spun their own yarn alright but they never said a word about the stealing of our property. One man giving evidence told so many lies that he was quite flushed and perspired profusely. Another witness was one whose life had been spared when he went on his knees, begging for mercy from the very men whose lives he was now trying to swear away.'[7]

On 11 March she was back in Belfast for her courtmartial which was conducted by four British officers. Her brother-in-law, John Mulligan of Lisconny, Riverstown arrived to testify for her at the trial. Again she was kept overnight in 'the odious Bridewell; but this time it was not quite so uncomfortable, as my solicitor had provided a mattress and blankets. I met the young man who had been sent down, probably by Diarmuid O'Hegarty and Mick Collins to defend me. I think he was Cecil Lavery. (In fact it was not Lavery but James C.R. Lardner B.L.).[8] The Dublin people wanted to keep me unknown and not identified with the movement.' This was probably the reason why she recognised the court and why in her written statement dated 11 March, the day of the courtmartial, she denied all involvement with the I.R.A. and said that she had simply given a lift to the three men who had been found in her car. She stuck to her story of forgetting her purse in the Harp and Shamrock in Sligo. She said she found it on the floor at the back of a chair in the dining room. Then she sat down, smoked a cigarette and leafed through the magazines and papers before leaving the hotel. About a half mile from the town her car stalled because of an airlock. While she was engaged in putting this matter right she was approached by eight or ten men who told her she would have to give some of them a lift. 'I was alone and I didn't like to object. They put some parcels in the car, which looked to me like groceries tied up in newspapers, and one bundle in white which looked like spades. This was the digging season in the locality. Three men joined the group and were at first challenged, and then after some conversation were told by the others to get into the motor-car. They did so and I started. We had gone a very short distance when we were held up by the military.' She claimed that she was and always had been a loyal and peaceable and law-abiding citizen.[9] In an attempt probably to portray herself as someone who was on good terms with the Unionist population she mentioned that she had been a nurse's attendant to O'Connor Morris and that he had left her £2,500 in his will. Included with her statement were three character references: from Sir John Irwin J.P. proprietor of Paper Manufacturers, 121, Upper Abbey St. Dublin; from J Maxwell Green J.P. puty Lieutenant for the County of Cavan; and from Major F. Fawcett of Nurney, Ballybrack, Co. Dublin. In his letter dated 21, February, 1921 Fawcett wrote:

Dear Miss Kearns,
My wife and I were much distressed to learn of your arrest

and it would give us the greatest pleasure to know that you could rebut any charge that may have been made against you. Your name was put on the mailing list for the massage staff, by your own request, at the Ministry of Pensions Special Surgical Hospital, Blackrock. You have nursed my wife admirably through a very critical illness, and of course you have nursed members of my wife's family and friends of ours. We have always had a high opinion of you personally and professionally and I sincerely wish you luck and an early acquittal.[10]

The courtmartial of the four accused opened with a request by Linda's counsel, Lardner, for a separate trial on the grounds that he wished to call Seamus Devins as a witness for the defence. The request was granted. Devins, Gilbride and Conway were not represented by counsel. They conducted their own defence.

The first prosecution witness in Linda's trial was Head Constable Timothy Murphy, nicknamed 'Spud' Murphy, who had beaten her in Sligo Barracks. He gave details of the arrest in which four lorries of military and police took part. Rifles were discovered in the back seat of the car and also in the folds of the hood. Field dressings and bandages were also found. Lardner questioned him closely about a whistle found in Linda's possession. Murphy said that in his opinion it was a police whistle but that he hadn't examined it closely. He agreed that some drivers used a whistle as a warning of approach and he wasn't able to say if Linda's car was fitted with a horn. The car permits were in order. Murphy was not questioned about striking Linda or about the confiscation of her personal property including her wristlet watch.

Sergeant Patrick Joyce, Constable John McCormick and Sergeant Michael Rourke who were involved in the Moneygold ambush, and Sergeant Michael Casey of Cliffoney Barracks gave evidence of identification of rifles and other items found in Linda's car. There was no cross examination of these witnesses. Constables Michael Barry,

Imprisonment

Edward Rennick and Thomas McLoughlin were the other witnesses apart from Head Constable Murphy who gave evidence regarding the arrest of Linda and the other accused. None admitted to using violence.

Seamus Devins was sworn in as the first witness for the defence. He told the court that he was on his way to Collooney to stay with a friend named Feeney. His own house had been burnt. Before the night of the arrest he had never met Linda nor had never heard her name. She was not in possession of arms on the night Gilbride, Conway and himself had been forced into Linda's car by a group of men, one of whom tossed a revolver onto the front seat. Under cross examination he said; 'I recognise the authority of this court. I also recognise the authority of the officer who administered the oath to me and its solemnity.'[11]

John Mulligan, Linda's brother-law,[12] said that he knew Linda for over fifteen years and that she had 'private means.' She had been a guest in his house and had been absent for only two days. 'As far as I know the accused has not been connected with any political organisation.... On the 20 November 1920 I was with the accused in Sligo.... I cannot say how she was dressed but I think she had a tweed suit on.'

Bernard Joseph O'Reilly of Cootehill, Co. Cavan was the next Defence witness.

'I am a chauffeur to Mr. Joseph Maxwell Green who is a Deputy Lieutenant of the county of Cavan. He has a shooting lodge in Co. Mayo near Bangor Erris. I was in the lodge with Mr. Green two years ago about this time. The accused was living in the neighbourhood then. She was carrying on nursing at her own expense amongst the poor. She had a motor car. She sold this car and got another. The car registration letters were IZ. The accused was acquainted with my master, Mr. Green. I remember meeting her when she had no horn on her car and she used the whistle now produced. The whistle originally belonged to a Captain...(surname indecipherable in manuscript). During the time I have known the accused I have never known her to be connected with an illegal association.'

After O'Reilly had given his evidence, Linda presented her written statement to the court and also spoke in her own defence. Then the Defence Counsel and the Prosecutor, Captain W.E Barron made their final addresses. The President of the court Major F.H. Shaw summed up the evidence and Linda was found guilty with the other three accused. She was brought back to Armagh Jail to await her sentence.[13]

A few weeks after the trial, Mrs Marie Mortished, secretary of The Irish Nurses' and Midwives' Union[14] wrote similarly worded letters to the Lord Lieutenant in Dublin and to Lloyd George the British Prime Minister asking that the courtmartial verdict on Linda be quashed or failing that, that the case be re-tried. She questioned the flimsiness of the evidence against Linda:

'no evidence appears to have been adduced to implicate Nurse Kearns with illegal acts or associations, the whole case against her resting on the fact that the arms etc. were found in a car belonging to, and driven by her. It is common knowledge that Nurses, in the pursuit of their calling, do not hesitate to avail of the kindly offices of the public in just such matters as the giving of a 'lift on the road', and it is only natural that the readiness of the public to help nurses should produce an instinctive reciprocal readiness on the part of a nurse to give help when asked... At the time of the arrest, the lamps of the car were alight, and there appears to have been no attempt on the part of the nurse at secrecy of any kind.'

Marie Mortished (née Sheilds) was a daughter of Adolphus Sheilds the well-known trade union activist and a sister of the actors Arthur and William Joseph Sheilds.[15] The latter was better known by his stage name Barry Fitzgerald. Marie was married to R.J.P. Mortished, a civil servant who was appointed first president of the Labour Court in 1946. The Irish Nurses' and Midwives' Union of which Marie was the first secretary was founded in Dublin in 1919 as a branch of the Irish Women's Workers' Union.

Maude MacCallum of Evelyn House, 62, Oxford Street, London also wrote one letter each, on Linda's behalf, to the Lord Lieutenant and to Sir Hamar Greenwood, Chief Secretary for Ireland. Both of the letters are identical in their wording and one paragraph is almost word for word the same as a section of Mrs Mortished's letter. Ms MacCallum said she was an Irish nurse. She concluded: 'Perhaps, Sir, you do not realise what the position of a woman would be, alone, at eleven o'clock at night, on a lonely road with three men who demanded a 'lift' in her car. At the very best, she risked being turned out and having to walk a long distance, and perhaps losing her car as well. I might say that I am a Unionist, and belong to a family of strong Unionist principles.' The Home Office on receipt of these letters, consulted with the R.I.C. authorities in Sligo and on the strength of the replies from Chief Inspector Neylon and District Inspector Russell it was decided that Linda's conviction should not be quashed.[16]

On 23 March, the Wednesday of Holy Week, Thomas Kearns, Linda's father died. She immediately set about getting parole to attend the funeral. The governor phoned Dublin Castle on her behalf. She waited all day on Good Friday for a favourable reply. Her request was denied. Instead, on that same day she was officially informed of the sentence handed down by the courtmartial—'Lorry loads of military came down from Belfast. They marched into the central hall of the gaol and lined up two deep making a formidable display of force. I was brought down by two wardresses and placed in the very middle between the two lines. A young officer stepped out and read me my sentence from a huge manuscript. It was a most impressive affair. The gist of it was that 'whereas and wherefore' I was found guilty on twenty six counts.' She was sentenced to ten years penal servitude and her car was confiscated. That night the governor instructed a wardress to sleep in Linda's cell and this arrangement continued till she left Armagh over a fortnight later.[17] Her co-accused Devins, Gilbride and Conway were given sentences of fourteen years each. The occupants of the first car who had been arrested on the same night as Linda and her friends, were, with the exception of Joe McDevitt, found not guilty and released. McDevitt was sentenced to two years hard labour.[18]

Kate O'Connell, Linda's sister, issued a statement on the sentence and on the death of their father:

'Ten years penal servitude and the confiscation of the motor car in view of the evidence given at the trial is a sentence that really caries its own comment. I know that my sister will not worry about the sentence. Whether it were 20 years or 10 it would be all the same. Nothing matters much and Linda will take her punishment as other innocent boys took a much harder sentence. But I fear what will worry her will be the fact that she was not with her poor father, whom she loved dearly, when he was dying and was not allowed out to be present at the last obsequies. At the very moment that she expected word with permission to attend the funeral an officer arrive to promulgate the sentence.'[19]

Meanwhile a plan of escape for Linda was devised in Dublin. On Sunday, 10 April, after mass, the curate informed her in the sacristy that on the following Wednesday, a fairday in Armagh, a rope would be thrown over the prison wall at a certain point which he indicated to her. She was to grab hold of it and would then be hauled over. Apart from mealtimes she was to remain in the grounds all day. The plan came to nothing however because on Tuesday, 12 April, an escort arrived in the prison to take her to the railway station where a number of well-wishers gathered to say goodbye to her. She hoped to be sent to Dublin to serve her sentence but instead she was taken Belfast. She now realised that her destination was some prison in England. A steamer conveyed Linda out of Belfast. She was told to travel steerage but was allowed on deck as soon as the ship was out of sight of land. The officer in charge informed her that she going to Walton Convict Prison at Liverpool where she arrived the next day. She says in her account:

> 'There was an all-pervading smell of raspberry jam from the adjoining factory. The first day I refused to put on the prison clothes. Canon St. John came in and told me that Madame Markievicz and others had been there and worn the clothes. He blessed them and I submitted to putting them on. I was weak and ill and felt unequal to a further struggle. The food was bad and the prison was dirty and badly kept. Every prisoner was locked up at 5 o'clock. You would have to be dying to be let out after that hour. We could not go to the lavatory, with the result that in the morning when the cells were opened there was a pestilential smell in the corridor. We were provided with a bucket in the cell.'

Canon St. John a convert to Catholicism was chaplain in Walton Prison. Linda had a very high regard for him. During the first three months of her term when she wasn't allowed letters it was arranged that they would be addressed to him. He then brought them in to her concealed in books. He kept her in touch with happenings at home by giving her a resume of the week's events after mass every Sunday. When as she says, 'terrible times of depression visited me, when I felt as if the shadow would never again be lifted from my life' he tried to keep up her spirits. Realising that it would be good for her to be occupied he asked her to embroider a set of altar cloths for him which she completed from patterns that he supplied.[20]

There were three categories of prisoners in Walton; First Offenders, Intermediates and Recidivists. Linda was placed in the latter category which included the prisoners convicted of murder, major robberies and other serious crimes. In *In Times of Peril* she says:

> 'Imagine the injustice of these English people who had my whole record and history before them, who knew my

character and the class to which I belonged, and who also knew, of course, that I had never been in prison before my arrest- imagine them placing me amongst the third class, the Recidivists. Nothing could have been more cruel or inhuman, for the very thought of the beings amongst whom my lot was cast was terrible to me.'[21]

Linda suffered a serious deterioration in her health resulting in periods of weakness and loss of weight. The prisoners were allowed one hour's exercise a day but towards the end of her time in Liverpool she couldn't walk for more than five minutes without taking a rest. She complained about the food but received no satisfaction. On one occasion, when she told the chairman of the prison committee that she had found a large worm in the cabbage served to her for dinner he said; ' Oh ! you got more than you were entitled to, then. Why, you got meat as well as vegetable!'[22] She was also extremely worried by the sanitary conditions in the prison and she refused to wash herself in the bath after seeing the evidence of venereal disease in it. In her letter requesting a transfer to a prison in Ireland she said there was only one lavatory for up to twenty five women and 'it is unfair to compel me to use the bath or lavatory used by women with diseases.' [23]

Linda spent at least one period of time in the prison hospital where she received extra milk and put on weight. She maintained that that the pint of milk she was allowed kept her alive in Walton. When the prison doctor decided that she no longer required it she 'broke down and cried before him, and I could not stop myself, although I was bitterly ashamed. I suppose he must have seen the state I was in, for he put me back on the milk again.'[24]

Linda's sister Kate O'Connell wrote to the prison authorities requesting permission to visit her. Linda was informed that a pass would be sent to her in Dublin. However the weeks went by and she was 'torn with anxiety, afraid that something had happened to prevent my sister from coming; and I knew too, that it would have to be a very serious thing which would keep her from coming over.' Eventually it transpired that the Deputy Governor, whom Linda despised, had never sent the pass.[25]

Sometime after Linda's arrival in Liverpool prison she was joined by another political prisoner from Ireland, Eileen McGrane. The authorities made every effort to keep them apart although they succeeded in making contact on a couple of occasions.[26] Eileen was transferred to Mountjoy Prison in Dublin and on 19 August (1921) Linda made her own formal request to be sent back to Ireland as well. The prison doctor was asked to comment on the request and he wrote the following report next day.-'The prisoner has complained of the food on a few occasions but only once has there been the slightest justification when the beans were not thoroughly cooked. I see her myself at least once a week and she has made no complaint nor mention of the sanitary arrangements. I do not know of any other prisoner being diseased or in any way unfit to use the same closet. Lavatory accommodation is adequate and kept in a clean condition. Her general health is good in my opinion. Imprisonment is not adversely affecting her health nor is it likely to do so. Her weight on reception was 134 pounds and present weight is 133 pounds.'[27] Later, an official from the Home office was sent down to interview her. For the meeting she was told to wear her Sunday garb which in addition to her prison clothes consisted of a white apron, a cap with frills and a white kerchief for her neck. The official's only comment as she listed her complaints was 'yes, yes.'[28] On 26 August, the Deputy–Governor of Walton informed the Home Office that Linda had met the Board of Visitors that day and that her petition was considered. They said she had no reasonable grounds for complaint.[29]

Marie Mortished wrote again on 29 August, saying that General Macready the commander-chief of the British forces in Ireland had given her union an assurance that when the country returned to normal conditions Linda's case might be reconsidered. The distance of the prison from her family made it impossible for her to get any visits 'as an interview of twenty minutes is scarcely worth the expense of a journey from Ireland. We earnestly request that you will be good enough to grant her the conditions of political prisoners and to have her removed to Dublin where she can have the advantage of such visits as she may be entitled to.' Mrs.Mortished's letter together with Linda's letter were sent by the Home Office to the Irish Office for comment but there is no record of a reply in Linda's prison file.[30] In any event, Linda decided to go on hunger strike and was taken to the prison hospital.[31] About ten days later she was informed that she was being transferred to Ireland.[32] It was commonly believed that the British authorities feared that she would die and that a woman martyr would have grave repercussions for the administration.

On 13 September a wardress from Mountjoy named Moore, accompanied by a small number of R.I.C. arrived in Walton to escort Linda back to Dublin.[33] They travelled by the night boat to Dún Laoghaire. Ms. Moore was very kind to her and gave her a bar of chocolate saying; 'it's real Irish chocolate and so you'll like it.' One of Linda's friends Josie O'Connor, was waiting for her on the pier. 'I fell into her arms with a cry of delight... she was horrified to see me looking so ill and hardly able to walk. With tears in her eyes she said: "Linda they have nearly killed you." I was brought to Mountjoy in a luxurious motor and got there just before dawn. The Chief Wardress was up and gave me some tea and bread and butter– the first real tea and real butter which I had tasted for nearly six months.'[34] Incidentally, Josie O'Connor would be waiting again for Linda outside the walls of the prison when four of the women made a bid for their freedom, about seven weeks later.

Chapter Five
Escape & Civil War

Within a couple of days of her arrival in Mountjoy Linda was in the prison hospital.[1] Her sister Kate visited her and subsequently told an *Irish Independent* reporter that although she had seen Linda only ten months before she hardly knew her such was the effect of prison life on her. She had lost weight and had a very bad cough. According to Kate, Linda, since childhood, had a weak chest and was very prone to illness. The medical officers in the prison were worried about her and in Kate's opinion the consequences for her health could be serious unless she was speedily released.[2]

Eileen McGrane, who was serving a four year sentence and Kathleen Brady a two year sentence, were also in hospital.[3] There were six other women political prisoners in Mountjoy at that time. These included Kathleen Burke, Aileen Keogh, Eithne Coyle and three young prisoners from Cork; Kate Crowley, aged 19, Madge Cotter, also 19 and Lily Cotter, aged 17. According to Linda the latter three were completely innocent of any crime. They had been thinning turnips in a field near where an ambush had taken place and were arrested although they had no involvement of any kind in the ambush and as far as she knew were not even members of Cumann na mBan.[4] Eileen McGrane is described in her prisoner file as Michael Collins' secretary. When she was arrested she was found to be in possession of six revolvers and a large quantity of dum dum ammunition. Also in the rooms occupied by her at 21 Dawson Street, Dublin 'was discovered a complete temporary office full of papers belonging to Michael Collins and plans for infecting army horses with glanders and introducing typhoid bacillus into the troops' milk.'[5] When Sir Hamar Greenwood Chief Secretary for Ireland gave this information in the House of Commons, a number of M.Ps said it was a concoction of Dublin Castle.

The Medical officer in Mountjoy Dr. B.J. Hackett, issued a report on Linda's health a week after her return to Dublin. Her weight on 11 March 1921 was 142 pounds but since that date she had lost 16 pounds. However, he considered her to be in fair health and 'organically sound.' He did confirm that she had a chronic cough for which she was being treated with the same prescription which her own specialist had given her before her arrest.[6] In her own account Linda wrote that this medicine was a syrup of coxelani compound.[7] In regard to the damage to her teeth which she had sustained in Sligo barracks, Linda lost no time in applying for treatment, at her own expense, from her dentist, Dan Doolin of 9 Fitzwilliam Square who in two written reports said that as a result of a blow she sustained when taken prisoner her front teeth were injured by dislocation, the upper central tooth in particular. 'There is a fifty per cent of repairing the damage done, in spite of the lapse of time since, if she was given the facilities for five or six visits to a dentist. In the patient's interest and in my own, I would not undertake the treatment of the case except in an equipped dental office.' He also reported that Frances Brady was in need of urgent dental treatment. Permission to leave the prison was granted to both prisoners on condition that a wardress in plain clothes accompany them to Mr. Doolin's surgery and that they return to Mountjoy after each visit. When C.A. Monroe the Governor conveyed this information to Linda she told him that 'she would be quite willing to give an undertaking to return to the prison but not if a wardress was sent with her; in that case she would give no undertaking. Miss Brady states the same.'[8] Monroe was well-regarded by Linda. She said of him and the medical men in Mountjoy that 'they lived up to the principle that everyone is entitled to his or her opinion, and did not think any the less of us because we had the courage of our convictions. They were undoubtedly gentlemen in the true sense of the word.'[9] The teeth episode was still going on when Linda made her successful bid for freedom.

Linda enjoyed much greater freedom in Mountjoy than in any of the other prisons in which she had been. The political prisoners were allowed to associate in the prison yard and the idea of escaping was frequently discussed. Linda suggested to Eileen McGrane that they should plan an escape but she and Kay Brady refused to get involved. Eileen advised Linda not to ask the three Cork prisoners as she considered them too young. Linda enlisted the help of Eithne Coyle and contact with the outside was established through Josie O'Connor and a young man called Seamus Burke, a native of Silvermines, who had been in jail in England with the patriot priest Fr. Dominic of Church Street. Josie brought a thermos flask into the prison and also a piece of dental wax. The wax was to be kept in the flask to ensure that it was soft enough to take the impression of a key which could then be supplied from outside. At least two of the wardresses cooperated with Linda and Eithne in getting impressions. Linda gives the name of one of them as Watters whereas Eithne says she was a girl from the West named Dillon. Another wardress, Dunne, also gave assistance.[10]

Seamus Burke arranged that they would escape across the prison wall at a point opposite the laundry wall and it was decided that four prisoners would make the break: Linda, Kathleen Burke, Aileen Keogh and Eithne Coyle. Between six and seven on the evening of 30 October a football match was organised by the women in the corridor which led out to the yard. Linda and her friends gradually edged their way towards the door at the end of the corridor. The other women, encouraged by Eileen McGrane, kept shouting noisily to distract the wardresses. Linda added to the din by shouting 'Up Sligo' as she scored a goal for her team.

The four women slipped through the corridor door which Linda opened with the duplicate key.

'We hid in the doorway of the laundry until the sentry who was on duty had passed to the other side of his round, which left us sufficient time to effect our escape. There was a revolving light on the corner of the wall which flashed intermittently and we succeeded in dodging that too. I threw a stone over the wall –I had been practising that for a week and was well able to it. A strong string with a piece of lead attached was thrown over to me. I called the other three and we started to pull, Unfortunately the string was cut by the sharp stones and the ladder fell back on the other side leaving me with a piece of lead in my hand. We all ran back to the laundry doorway and waited until the sentry had passed again. I went back to the wall and threw another stone over it. I got the string back again, this time with a knife attached. We all pulled carefully and well out from the wall. This time the ladder came down with a flop.'

The women had decided that Linda, because she was serving the longest sentence, would go first. Eithne Coyle held the ladder out from the wall to make the ascent as easy as possible but as the last to go herself she suffered severe scrapes and bruises to her hands. Linda reached the top of the wall and grabbed the rope which had been made from window cord. Her friend Josie O'Connor whispered up to her; 'slither, Linda, slither.' She slipped down the dangling rope to the ground and was quickly put on a motor-bike driven by I.R.A. man Tim Ryan. According to Linda, Ryan was a friend of Mick Collins 'and must have been one of his squad because he had a motor-bike belonging to them.' He brought her to Berkley Road where the writer and poet Dr. Oliver St.John Gogarty was waiting for her. Ryan told Gogarty that another of the escapees was expected to arrive shortly but if she didn't turn up within three minutes he was to leave with Linda only. Almost immediately, however Kathleen Burke arrived with a Fianna Éireann boy named Donnelly. Dr. Gogarty drove the two women by a roundabout route to Earlsfort Terrace where he took them into the house of Miss O'Rourke, a relation of his wife. After he dressed Linda's hands which had been cut when she slid down the rope, he left to find out what had happened to Aileen

Keogh and Eithne Coyle. He returned some time later to say that they had gotten away and were safe in the house of Dr. McLafferty. Miss O'Rourke was extremely kind to Linda and Kathleen providing them with 'hot coffee, baths and she put us to bed in the most lovely bedroom. I never realised before what a lovely feel a satin eiderdown has, and how restful and soothing ironed linen sheets are.'

Before they left Miss O'Rourke's, Gogarty, who had a marvellous sense of fun, coaxed Linda into applying for the vacant position of matron in the Meath Hospital on headed notepaper from the Shelbourne Hotel. He instructed her on what to write emphasising in particular her vast experience of British institutions! 'Although Dr. Gogarty had the courage to propose me under my name, he found no seconder, but I am certain he got a great kick out of the whole situation, especially when he saw the British military raiding the Shelbourne Hotel the following day.' Gogarty also met Andrew Cope the assistant under-secretary for Ireland whom he mocked for 'not being able to hold his women.' Cope assured him that they would soon be caught because they wouldn't be able to resist the attractions of the Grafton Street shops.[11]

After Linda found out that there was a reward for their capture she made contact with Eithne Coyle and Aileen Keogh and they decided to leave Dublin. Aileen went back to Gorey where she worked as a housekeeper for Rev. Fr. Sweetman. Fr. Sweetman had a school in Gorey. Dr. McLaverty arranged with Joseph O'Connor, a Circuit Court Judge in Cork to take the other three women to the Convent of the Cross and Passion in Kilcullen. They were there about a week when Tim Ryan arrived late one night on his motor-bike with the news that the British authorities knew of their whereabouts. Michael Collins had discovered that Seamus Burke, tempted by the reward, had betrayed them. The I.R.A. later forced Burke to leave the country.

Linda contacted the local curate in Kilcullen whom she had met in the convent and who was a sympathiser. He drove the three women to Duckett's Grove in Carlow, the house attached to an I.R.A training camp. 'The house itself was a beautiful residence, fully furnished. We had our rooms and also a dining room allotted to us by the officer in charge, and orderlies to wait on us.' Liam Stack, a native of Listowel was the officer in charge. He afterwards became a Garda superintendent. Linda undertook to supervise the housekeeping arrangements in the camp and she also organised a small first aid hospital which was of very practical benefit for eleven prisoners who having escaped from Kilkenny jail by tunnel arrived in the camp on foot in an exhausted condition.

A short time after the three women had taken up residence the local parish priest paid a visit. 'He was shocked at the idea that three women would remain where there were so many men. I explained to him that I was a trained nurse and that there were nurses in charge of the hospitals in every army in the world and that I saw nothing wrong in remaining there. We won him round to our point of view.' Concerts were organised to keep up the morale of the men who numbered in all about four hundred.[12]

Security was stepped up in Mountjoy after the escape. The women political prisoners, McGrane, Brady, Crowley an the two Cotters were subjected to what was described as a 'vindictive policy' against them Three armed auxiliaries continually watched them- a situation which they found intolerable and which they responded to by going on hunger strike and by refusing to leave their cells.

Linda's escape from Mountjoy was celebrated in verse by Michael Daly of New York.

> *While we sing the glory of the sons of Erin*
> *And the deeds of valour of her gallant boys,*
> *We can't forget noble Linda Kearns*
> *That led the trio o'er Mountjoy's old walls;*
> *She was a flower of the rarest beauty,*
> *From Sligo's valleys down by the sea,*
> *Who gladly answered the call of duty,*
> *As Ireland fought that she might be free.*

Linda (right) and her sister Nora as students in Beirlegem, C 1903

Catherine Kearns, Linda's mother

Linda in Baggot Street uniform with her father

Linda's Sister Nora as a nurse

Thomas Clarke, Linda's Uncle

Back Row: 4th from left; Tommy Goff. 2nd from left; Charles McGarry (Linda's Brother in law)
Second Row: 3rd from left; Daisy McGarry (Linda's Sister) 5th from left; Linda
Seated: 3rd from left; Mrs. Tom Clarke, 4th from left; Jack O'Connell, 5th from left; Kate O'Connell, 6th from left; Thomas Clarke

Linda (on right) with friends in Duckett's Grove, Carlow, December 1921

Linda in Duckett's Grove, 1921

Muriel McSwiney

Linda in America

Kathleen Barry (left) and Linda in Australia

Linda, Kathleen Barry and Friends

Left to right: Frank Aiken, Linda, Eamonn de Valera, Margaret Pearse, Oscar Traynor

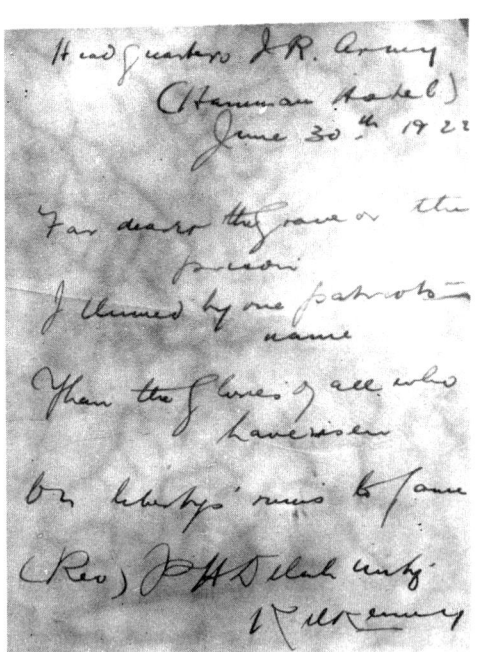

Autographs of Republican activists during the Civil War

A White Cross nurse was her occupation;
She nursed the wounded, the weak and low,
And the gallant soldiers of the Irish nation
Who for their country did strike a blow.
But the Black and Tans with a rattling sabre
Did put and end to her charity,
And sentenced her to ten years' hard labour,
Because she believed in an Ireland free.

At first the villains were going to shoot her,
But then decided to have her tried;
They knew full well if they 'd execute her,
Themselves might pay with their precious lives.
For on Erin's soil were a band of heroes,
The grandest soldiers in all history,
Who might not forget to pay back the debt,
As they now were out to make Ireland free.

With three more colleens she lay imprisoned-
Miss Burke, Miss Keogh and Miss Coyle so gay;
So back to freedom their thoughts they turned
Led on by Linda from Knocknarea.
With ropes for ladders they scaled the walls
And snapped their fingers at tyrrany,
As Linda Kearns that child of Erin,
With her gallant comrades once more was free.

Some effects of prison life remained with Linda for years to come. For example she could not or would not lock a door even when she went on holidays. This was at variance with the usual practice of women when they stayed in hotels on their own. Another of her characteristics, which may have come from her prison experience or from being years on the run, was her custom of always sitting with her back to a wall in a public place, such as a restaurant, where she had a full view of the room.[13]

Linda left Duckett's Grove after the signing of the Anglo-Irish treaty on 6 December 1921. She followed the lead of de Valera in opposing the settlement which established the 26 county Irish Free State as a self-governing dominion within the British Commonwealth. The Treaty was ratified by Dáil Éireann on 7 January, 1922 and by the British Parliament on 31 March. The vote in the Dáil was 64 votes to 57. A week after the ratification Linda was back with her sister, Annie Mulligan, in Lisconny, Collooney, Co. Sligo. The local Volunteers and Sinn Féin clubs staged a celebration in her honour on Saturday, 14 January. According to the *Sligo Champion* ...

> 'the district was ablaze. Every house was lit up; bonfires blazed on the hills, and young and old turned out to pay respect to one who stood up for them in the terrible days just past. The fife and drum bands of Riverstown and Sooey led the Volunteer companies of their respective districts. The Carrickbanagher Company of Volunteers also made a fine display. The scene was a grand one as Miss Kearns arrived and passed between lines of Volunteers, the blazing torches lighting up the roads and fields around.'

Brian Flannery, chairman of Riverstown Sinn Féin club presided and the address was read by Edward Mc Loughlin. He acknowledged Linda's contribution to the struggle for independence; 'We gladly acclaim that great change was brought about by you and your compatriots. We trust the rising nation will appreciate your worth and we pray that you and your brave associates will now work more diligently than ever to crown this old land with the diadem of peace and prosperity.' The address was signed by Brian Flannery, John McGann, Michael Connolly, Mark Quigley and Edward McLoughlin. Linda thanked everybody for what she said was an unexpected reception. However, privately she was not pleased with the tone of the address which she felt was decidedly pro-Treaty.[14]

Early in 1922 also, Linda in collaboration with the author Annie M.P. Smithson, wrote the account of her involvement in the period 1916-1921 *'In Times of Peril'*

Leaves From the diary of Nurse Linda Kearns from Easter Week 1916 to Mountjoy, 1921.' This slim volume which was written in a matter of weeks was published by The Talbot Press, Dublin. Unfortunately, but understandably it omits the names of several personalities involved with Linda in the campaign. It is written in an effusive and at times sentimental tone which mars the importance of the subject matter. In later years Linda grew to dislike it so intensely that several of her friends sensing her unease, frequently went out of their way to annoy her by praising the work to the skies! She particularly hated the photograph of herself on the cover.[15] Nevertheless *In Times of Peril* is a prized possession of surviving members of her family.

Annie Smithson would have been known to Linda through the Irish Nurses' Union and possibly from her association with Cumann na mBan for whom she worked in a nursing capacity. She converted to catholicism in 1907 and later became involved in the republican movement. She was imprisoned but released when she went on hunger strike. In the 1920s she became an influential figure in nursing circles and was elected secretary of the Irish Nurses' Organisation in 1929. Annie was very catholic and conservative in outlook and she with other nursing leaders of like mind, contributed to undermining the voices of more liberal and progressive women in the nursing world.[16]

On 14 April an anti-Treaty force under Rory O'Connor seized the Four Courts in Dublin and remained in possession until it surrendered on 30 June. Meanwhile the result of the Irish Free State election in June gave the pro-Treaty group 58 seats and the anti-Treaty group 36. Labour secured 17 seats and the remaining 17 were divided between the Farmers and Independents.

Linda's involvement in the Civil War began on 28 June when the pro-Treaty forces commenced their bombardment of the Four Courts. She and Muriel MacSwiney, the widow of Terence tried to get into the building to assist the republicans inside but since the fire was already blazing they were not allowed to pass. Incidentally this was the first time Muriel and Linda had met. Both women then made their way to Barry's Hotel the headquarters of the Republican forces which had not yet come under heavy attack. According to Muriel, 'Linda was in charge of the Red Cross hospital in Barry's with several other nurses and doctors and she managed everything most efficiently. She was indefatigable in her attention to the boys in Barry's Hotel and also in the hotels in O'Connell's Street to which the general headquarters was removed on Friday 29th.' Muriel said that she was terrified at first 'but fear soon completely left me.'[17]

Linda Kearns also displayed a degree of courage during the fighting that took place between anti-Treaty and pro-Treaty forces, June 30 - July 5, 1922 in O'Connell's Street, which was widely recognised. For example while in the Hammam Hotel, she went to the assistance of a pro-Treaty soldier who was lying wounded in the street. She did this with the permission of her commanding officer Cathal Brugha and she was by Brugha's side when he himself fell mortally wounded.[18]

The grim events in O'Connell Street were not without their lighter moments however. One such arose from Linda's attempt to make cocktails for the besieged garrison. She together with Muriel MacSwiney and Kathy Barry, sister of Kevin Barry, headed for the deserted cocktail bar and set to work. Several disparate drinks were merged and then one of the girls said; 'Don't they always put the white of an egg in a cocktail?' The kitchen was raided and the final vital ingredient was added. After declaring that the drink was 'a lovely colour' they returned in triumph to their comrades one of whom on tasting the concoction suggested that they take it out to the Free Staters where it could prove lethal![19]

According to Linda 'when the various groups were ordered out of the Gresham, some going with De Valera, and some with Madam Markievicz, there remained only 16 men with Cathal Brugha, Dr. Brennan, Art O'Connor, Kathy Barry, Muriel MacSweeney and myself. We held the place for two days after the rest had gone.' Then Brugha asked Art O'Connor to lead Kathy, Muriel and the sixteen men out of the hotel. Once outside they were captured. Linda was allowed to remain. She had a conversation alone with Brugha about two hours before he was shot. 'I asked him was he acting wisely in going to his death. We have too many unnecessary deaths already', I said. He replied, 'Civil War is so serious that my death may bring its seriousness home to the Irish people. I feel that if it put a stop to the Civil War it would be a death worthwhile.' Linda was by his side when he moved to a back door of the hotel. The two of them went out into a back lane. Brugha had a revolver in each hand and he kept shouting 'no surrender.' He was shot in the hip and the femoral artery was severed. Linda was not hit. In her opinion it was not the intention of the Free State soldiers to kill him and so they aimed low. 'But as he was a small man he was struck higher than they expected.' Linda travelled in the ambulance with him to the Mater Hospital all the while holding the artery between her finger and thumb. She maintained that he had not lost a great deal of blood before being admitted but that it was up to an hour before he was taken to the theatre and another hour before a doctor arrived. She herself fainted and the same ambulance that had taken Brugha to the Mater brought her back to her own home in Gardiner Place. Brugha died two days later on 7 July. Linda drove out to Brittas and brought Harry Boland in to the funeral. When it was over she drove him part of the way to Skerries.[20] Three weeks later Boland himself was dead, shot by Free State troops.[21]

Shortly after the O'Connell Street fighting Linda was involved in another incident which Cathal O'Shannon recalled in 1951. 'On the evacuation of the Gresham, Hammam and Granville one party of anti-Treaty people set out by motor car for Sligo to join up with local forces and other groups from Dublin. This party included the late Annie M.P. Smithson, nurse and novelist; two other ladies; a gentleman named Walsh; Mr A.W.G. Smyllie; Dr.

Holmes Ievers –these two were students in Trinity College at the time– and a driver. At Mullingar they were held up by Free State forces and very definitely they were in the gravest danger until next day Nurse Kearns hurried from Dublin to their rescue– she took Mrs. Terence MacSwiney with her in the expectation that that honoured name would receive rapid passage through Free State obstacles – and certified that they were a Red Cross unit. On her representations the ladies were released and if the men came through with their lives they were sent on as prisoners to Dundalk Jail. From there very soon they made their escape through a big hole blown in the jail wall by forces under the command of Commandant Frank Aiken.'[22]

Muriel MacSwiney was one of those who visited Harry Boland before he died of his wounds in the Mater Hospital on 1 August. Then, literally within days, she and her new friend Linda Kearns were on their way to America on a fund-raising tour.

Chapter Six
America & Australia 1922-25

In her own account Linda says that it was Éamon de Valera who sent herself and Muriel MacSwiney to America to raise funds.[1] This is in conflict with the statement of Kathleen Boland, sister of Harry who wrote that they went on their own initiative.[2] In any event Linda and Muriel set out for Cork and were waiting for their ship while the city was under attack from the Free State forces. They travelled first to Cardiff under assumed names accompanied by Robert Briscoe, later a Fianna Fáil T.D. and Lord Mayor of Dublin. From there they went by train to Euston Station in London and stayed for a short time in the flat of one of Briscoe's friends in Holborn.[3] They sailed from Britain in the first week of August 1922. Briscoe met them again in the U.S. and they were later joined by Kathleen Boland and by Hanna Sheehy Skeffington, widow of Francis Sheehy-Skeffington who though a pacifist had been shot in cold blood by a British army officer in 1916. Others to come out later included Fr. Michael O'Flanagan, Kathleen Brady, Máire Comerford and J.J. Kelly (Sceilg). It was Muriel MacSwiney's second visit to the United States. She had gone there in late 1920, a few weeks after her husband's death. On this 1922 tour she spent a much shorter time in America than the other women.

Back in Sligo while Linda was on her way to the U.S., Free State troops began to close in on the republicans led by two of Linda's friends Seamus Devins and Billy Pilkington. Devins had been elected a Sinn Féin T.D. in the June general election. In an engagement on Benbulben mountain on 20 September, six republicans were shot dead. Devins was among the slain. The other five were: Brian MacNeill, Joseph Banks, Patrick Carroll, Harry Benson and Tommy Langan.[4]

In one of her first speeches of the tour, that in Lexington Theatre, New York, Linda said that she and Mrs MacSwiney had come to America for two reasons: 'To tell the truth about the state of affairs in Ireland and to appeal for the dependents of these brave men who are fighting and who have fought and who are in jail for the freedom of our country. She stressed a number of points that she would repeat many times throughout the tour including England's influence over the world press, the flaws in the Treaty such as the oath of allegiance, the retention of certain ports, and the position of the governor-general. 'Ireland has not got freedom. That is only the beautiful illustrated cover of a very vile book. We have a saying in the West of Ireland, never take the book by the cover. I say to you, don't take the Treaty by the cover.'

In the section of the speech dealing with the dependents she instanced the case of Cathal Brugha's widow and children and also the wife and mother of Garry Houlihan. Houlihan had fought with her in O Connell Street. She also mentioned the 'big Tipperary man' whose wife had died during the Black and Tan War. He had walked to Dublin to take part in the fighting on the republican side, leaving his children in the care of his mother. She also appealed on the grounds that some of the prisoners were in great need of medical attention:

> 'I have an appeal for the boys themselves. This appeal is very dear to my heart. These boys got hurt and wounded. They want treatment, medical and surgical. They have had legs and arms taken off and they want artificial limbs. They want massage, electric treatment, and skin grafting; all expensive treatment. There are no free hospitals in Ireland today. We must pay from $15 to $20 a week for a bed. I want funds for these boys. I want to be able to say when I come back that America has given funds for these cases. I want to be able to visit the boys who had their limbs taken off and say to them 'I have funds for artificial limbs that America has given to me.'[5]

A couple of days later Linda and Muriel began their series of meetings in cities and towns of Massachusetts.[6] An organising committee of 100 members representing 600 Irish societies in the state had been formed a short time previously to supervise the arrangements for the tour. This committee was chaired by Patrick J O'Hegarty with Mrs Frank Scanlon vice-chairman, Miss Elizabeth Needham, secretary and Peter Hartnett, treasurer. The two women arrived by train in Boston to a huge welcome. About 500 led by Mrs Frank Scanlon were on hand to greet them. A group of ex-service men carrying the Irish and American flags led the way, followed by a long string of cars, from the South Station to the Copley Plaza Hotel. In reply to a question from one of the reporters who visited the hotel they both insisted that as far as republicans were concerned the Treaty had in no way altered the situation in Ireland. Muriel MacSwiney was asked what would be the effect on the drive for funds of the statement of Dr. Michael Curley, archbishop of Baltimore, in which he denounced the men and women of America 'who are sending money and munitions to De Valera and his followers.' She replied: 'The people who will give their money to help Ireland keep her Republic will understand Archbishop Curley's statement. We never had the bishops of Ireland with us either you know…this has nothing to do with our religion. We are staunch Catholics in Ireland. But a bishop's political opinions can have no greater weight than the political opinions of anyone else.' Linda agreed and went on to deal with another quotation from Curley's statement i.e. that American benefactors of the republican cause in Ireland were as guilty of murder as were the men who shot Michael Collins. She said that Collins was not murdered but that he had died during a battle in which he had fought for an hour and ten minutes before being hit.[7] Dr. Michael Curley was on a visit to Ireland when he criticized those opposing the Treaty. He arrived in Dublin on 19 August accompanied by his friend, the singer John McCormack. Referring to De

Valera, Curley said: 'When he came to America I was his friend and I presided over his big meeting at Jacksonville, Florida. Now as an Irishman with things as they are, I can no longer see eye to eye with him.'[8]

The two women had their hair 'prettily bobbed' and donned long, clinging, silken gowns 'that bespeak the boulevards of Paris' for the meeting in Symphony Hall, Boston, which was attended by over 4,000. They were escorted up the main aisle of the hall by a bodyguard of ex-service men and they were visibly astonished by the ovation they received. As they took their seats on the platform each was presented with a large bouquet of yellow chrysanthemums. The *Soldiers' Song* was sung before the speeches began. Muriel MacSwiney spoke only briefly but Linda delivered what was described as 'a brilliant speech which brought the audience to its feet several times.' The crowd cheered loudly when the name of Eamon de Valera was mentioned. A few in the audience booed the name of Michael Collins whereupon Linda stopped and said, 'Collins is dead now. Keep silence.' She went on to describe some of her own experiences in the fighting and the effect of warfare on the people. 'It hurt me more to see the thatched cottages of the west of Ireland burned than it did to see all the big houses in Dublin go', she declared. She reiterated what she had said in New York regarding the influence of the English Press.

Thomas O'Connor, described as an officer of the Republican Army, also spoke. The meeting was chaired by Attorney John F Hughes of Boston and two other prominent personalities present were J.L. Madden of Brooklyn, New York, the organiser of the tour; and Frank F Walshe. Pledges of $100 to $1000 by various Irish societies were given and the response from the audience was extremely generous. The members of the reception committee were: Mrs Frank C Scanlon, Miss Elizabeth M Needham (State Vice-President of The Association for the Recognition of an Irish Republic- (A.A.R.I.R), Peter J Harnett, Miss M E Burke, Miss M Golden, Mrs Barbara McCarthy and Martin

Hunt. Except for John Hughes, who supervised the collection, all the officials at the meeting were women.[9]

In New Bedford, Massachusetts on 12 October Muriel MacSwiney began her address in Irish. She told the meeting that the 'deprivation of our language is one of the most terrible things we have suffered from the enemy.' Elizabeth Needham said that Ireland would not be subdued and characterised De Valera as the 'the George Washington of Ireland.' Linda declared that she always had two ambitions: to visit America and to see the British Empire smashed before she died. 'I am seeing America now and I hope to get my other wish while I am still alive.'[10]

Speaking in Albany, Linda and Hanna Sheehy-Skeffington, who arrived in America in late October, criticized the prison conditions which republican prisoners were subjected to and also the military tribunals which were handing down sentences. Linda said that the jails 'are wholly worse than the worst America has ever had' and in her condemnation of the military courts Mrs. Sheehy-Skeffington declared: 'Men that are tried for offences are not tried by jury for in the Free State government: there is no such thing as trial by jury anymore. They are tried by secret military tribunals, the members of which are enemies to the defendants. I know this because I am a judge in Ireland myself.' She said that there were about six thousand republican prisoners who had some twenty thousand dependents for whose upkeep a sum of $5000 per week was required. The Free State government did not permit her committee 'to insert even paid advertisements in English newspapers requesting aid for these dependents.' She went on to say that 'there are only two parties in Ireland: the party that is for England and the party that is for Ireland. The Free Staters are for England and the Republicans are for Ireland.'[11] In a letter, dated 6 November, to Annie P. Smithson Linda regretted the fact that ' Mrs S.S. must be back in Ireland for Xmas. She is a very clever woman and it will be hard to find a substitute.'¹² Linda's admiration for Hanna Sheehy Skeffington was not shared by Robert Briscoe. In his book *'For the Life of Me'* he says that although she had played an important part in the War of Independence, 'she had also acquired a great opinion of herself, which was not completely reciprocated by the Irish-Americans.' Apparently she was deeply suspicious of well known Washington lawyer John Finerty, national president of the A.A.R.I.R. whom she believed to be disloyal to the republican cause and to be exerting a bad influence on Muriel MacSwiney. It was Sheehy Skeffington's opinion that Finerty should be shot and she asked Briscoe to go to Washington to investigate him. Linda travelled with Briscoe from New York. He felt that Linda 'although a true heroine was not the sort of girl who looked right for the part. Tall and bony she was, with a long face and awkward ways.' In any event they interviewed Finerty in his office and Briscoe quickly came to the conclusion that Sheehy Skeffington's suspicions were unfounded. Finerty told them that Muriel MacSwiney was staying with his wife at their country house in Virginia. When he was informed of Hanna's accusations he decided to travel back to New York and confront her. 'Mrs Skeffington and all her crowd, including Dynamite Mike Kelly, were waiting in her apartment in the old Park Avenue Hotel for me to bring back word of what had happened to Finerty. You should have seen their faces when I walked in with the corpse on my arm.

'Why, John, how wonderful to see you,' says Mrs. Skeffington.

But John was not having it. He spoke his piece; and we cleared that little matter up in a hurry.'¹³

Hanna also wrote a letter, which was intercepted by the Provisional Government, to Áine O'Rahilly in Ireland concerning Muriel's behaviour. She said that Muriel had...

> '... broken several engagements for us, refused to attend receptions, left hotel in Philadelphia where L[inda] and K[athleen] were and so on. She is with an unscrupulous crowd who use her and exploit her ....This group are try-

ing to get us up against the U.S. so as to have us deported or at any rate discredited...... Now can you get her recalled by Chief, Austin [Stack] or Mary [MacSwiney].....Mary Mac would help us I think as she was up against this before and knows conditions.'[14]

On 18 November Linda and her friends learned of the fate of James Fisher, Peter Cassidy, Richard Twohig and John Gaffney, the first republicans to be executed by order of the Free State Government.[15] They had been put to death the previous day. Kathleen Boland who with the other women addressed a meeting in New York on the 18th, wrote in her diary:

'We heard of the executions of those four brave boys. We could hardly speak with sorrow.'[16]

A few days later the execution of Erskine Childers and the imprisonment and hunger strike of Mary MacSwiney sister of Terence MacSwiney resulted in a mass demonstration by republican sympathisers on Seventh Avenue and Fiftieth Street, New York, outside the Earl Carroll theatre where Linda and Muriel were due to speak. Childers was executed on 24 November 1922 and the New York protest which was organised by the American Association for the Recognition of the Irish Republic (A.A.R.I.R) took place two days later. The doors of the theatre were opened shortly before 8p.m. and within 15 minutes the auditorium was packed. 'Crowds continued to arrive on every trolley car, elevated train and subway.' Unable to gain admittance to the theatre, the crowd decided to hold a meeting outside. American flags and banners protesting at English policy in Ireland were on display and an effigy of King George V was burned. A ladder was hoisted in Fiftieth Street and the speakers used it as a platform. The police were unsuccessful in their attempts to break up the meeting. In fact when they came under attack they deemed it prudent to return to their stations in taxicabs.[17]

In her letter to Annie P. Smithson Linda referred to the imprisoning of Mary MacSwiney: 'I see in today's paper that Mary MacSwiney is arrested and on hunger strike.... The hunger strike may mean a great deal to our cause. I do not suppose that any government could look on and see a repetition of Terence MacSwiney's death but of course some governments are capable of anything.'[18] Mary MacSwiney was freed on 27 November. Linda received word of the release while addressing a meeting in Atlantic City. She told the wildly cheering crowd that 'Mary MacSwiney's release is one of our biggest victories. She has won her victory and we will win ours.'[19] On another occasion Linda described Mary MacSwiney as 'the brains of the Irish Republic.'[20]

It was in Worcester, Massachusetts that Linda came face to face with the man who informed the authorities of her whereabouts after her escape from Mountjoy. At a meeting in the Mechanics Hall which was chaired by Miss Jennie H Quinn, national director of the A.A.R.I.R, Linda was describing her escape from Mountjoy when the audience was puzzled to see her walk close to the edge of the platform and adjust her glasses. For a moment she appeared to lose the thread of her speech as she stared in a particular direction. In the Bankcroft Hotel later, she explained what happened.

'I was startled for an instant, when I saw sitting there in the audience, four rows back from the platform, a man whose face I can never forget. He was the man who helped me to escape from the prison. A price was placed on my head. The money tempted this man and he led a party of the enemy soldiers to the convent where I was taken in. He left Ireland soon after. I did not know that he had come to America but there he sat. It was not a case of mistaken identity. I knew him and he knew me. I hold no grudge against him now. He was young. He did me a good turn and later was tempted by English gold as many another has been. Yes, Seamus Burke is in Worcester and is ashamed of himself.'

She said that Burke had been forced to leave the country by the I.R.A.[21]

In an interview with a newspaper reporter in Buffalo's Lafayette hotel, Linda spoke of the educational advantages enjoyed by American children, which were in stark contrast to the schools' situation in Ireland. America provided free libraries, free education and its schools were modern whereas in Ireland 'our children carry turf to school to keep them from freezing. There are no free books thanks to England.' She declared that she was 'an unmitigated rebel' who could find no words strong enough to express her pent-up feelings against the English administration in Ireland. The reporter described Linda as 'a young, pretty, flaming creature– T.N.T. wrapped in tissue paper with a blue ribbon wound about.'[22] Incidentally, at one particular meeting, her reference to carrying turf to school proved an embarrassment to her own cousin Matha Clarke who had emigrated sometime previously. He told her privately afterwards that 'she needn't have bothered mentioning it.'[23]

As the tour progressed Linda became the dominant speaker at meetings. She usually spoke for upwards of an hour and her popularity seemed to derive from her attraction to the audience as the woman who had seen active service over an extended period of time. Undoubtedly she also possessed an easy speaking style combined with a pleasant personality. According to one observer: 'She spoke rapidly, her words being broken up into short phrases with brief pauses in between. She smiled much of the time even when she was delivering her sharpest shafts.' Another commentator wrote that 'she possesses in liberal quantities Irish wit and Irish spirit.' She spoke in what was described as a cultured Dublin accent only occasionally reverting to a west of Ireland mode of speech. There appears to have been a definite strategy adopted by Hanna Sheehy Skeffington, Kathleen Boland and Linda in their addresses to the various meetings. Kathleen usually made a short speech and concentrated on the circumstances of her brother Harry's death and the continuing involvement of her family in the armed struggle. Harry's popularity with Irish-American leaders from his days on tour with de Valera ensured a deep sympathy from audiences. Hanna dealt with various aspects of the political situation in Ireland, particularly the military courts while Linda concentrated on such topics as the killings during the Civil War, the treatment of republicans in the Irish prisons, her own involvement in the War of Independence and her abhorrence of the Treaty. She was particularly scathing of Richard Mulcahy whom she dubbed 'the greatest traitor of them all.'[24] She also disliked the use of the term Irregulars to describe the republicans and was at pains to demonstrate its inaccuracy as far as she was concerned.[25] In a number of speeches she castigated Tim Healy, the Governor-General of the Free State and a barrister by profession, who, she said refused to defend Roger Casement who had been hanged in August 1916. Healy had 'never impressed the rank and file of the Irish people with his sincerity. Numerous instances were on record to prove that his interest in Ireland's welfare was not genuine but prompted by a desire for prestige in the eyes of English officials.' Linda also claimed that Healy had declined to act as her counsel at her own courtmartial in March, 1921. 'She will hang. There is no use fighting for her', was his comment.[26]

Chicago was one of the cities that the women's delegation found extremely generous and welcoming.[27] It was also the city where a top-ranking member of the Catholic hierarchy spoke to the women and pledged his support for an Irish Republic. According to Kathleen Boland 'the money poured in like water' in Chicago. Linda spoke a number of times in this city on two separate visits in 1923 –the first in January/February and the second in April/May. On 22 January, in the Orchestra Hall she predicted that an Irish Republic would be established before the end of the year. Two of the main organisers of the visits to Chicago were Angela de Gann and the much respected Mrs. Mary MacWhorter, chairperson of the Women's Auxiliary of the A.O.H. who had come to Ireland the previous summer and had spoken to Harry Boland among others. She had campaigned in previous years against the introduction of conscription into Ireland and also for the recognition of the right of Ireland to freedom and self-determination at the International Peace Conference after the First World War. It was Mrs MacWhorter who introduced Linda and the other women to Archbishop Mundelein of Chicago. He told them that he was glad to see them on their own account but also because he wanted to send a special message to Éamon de Valera. He asked them to tell Mr. de Valera that 'he had the same friendship that he had three years ago, that he believed in him, had faith in him and prayed for him. The archbishop subscribed $100 to the Dependents' Fund. Mrs. MacWhorter gave a similar amount.

Linda and Kathleen Boland were back in Chicago the following April. In a letter to one of the newspapers Linda expressed her pleasure at meeting old friends again.

> Morrison Hotel,
> Chicago,
> May 8, 1923.

Since our departure from Chicago last February, Kathleen and I have looked forward with pleasure to our return here, and on occasions when we met with difficulties, as one does on a tour like ours, we always said to each other 'never mind, Chicago will make up for all this.' We arrived here on April 28th. A crowd of dear good friends met us at the station, and we both felt that we were 'coming home.' I heard one dear big-hearted woman who arrived late ask 'have they come?.' It sounds cold on paper but it meant so much- there was love and welcome in the question. Girl friends were there with large bouquets of flowers and candies. One of these dear girls found out on my last visit here that I have a partiality for hard candy and there she was with a box of my favourites and she is at every meeting we go to with the same.(Angela dear, I can't eat them all, a smaller box would do)

Our first meeting was at the invitation of the Napper

Tandy and Michael Fitzgerald Council. I promised one of these indefatigable workers of the Napper Tandy, when here in February that I would wear my uniform on my return, if I put on weight and got strong enough to carry it. Your beautiful American climate has done that for me and I am now strong enough to carry all the heavy trappings a uniform entails....... .The meeting of the Napper Tandy and Michael Fitzgerald council was splendid. The generosity of their members for the past four months has been taxed so much that I had qualms of conscience appealing again for funds for the relief of women and children in Ireland.... But I need not have worried. They gave again and did not need appealing to. The large sum of $602 was subscribed and forwarded next day, and has reached the people who need it ere this.

Linda went on to say that a further $600 had been raised by other Irish groups in Chicago. Incidentally, the largest sums subscribed by individuals on this tour, apart from those already mentioned were: $100 each from Mayor Curley of Boston, Judge Richard Campbell of New York and the Hon. James K. McGuire of Syracuse, New York. $250 was donated by the Hon. Frank P. Walsh of New York and $225 by Leo McSweeney of Rochester, New York. At the end of the first six months of the tour over $100,000 had been collected. Linda explained that the money raised was sent to a central office in Dublin. Each county had its own sub-office to which details of dependents' needs were relayed. Funds were then allocated based on the information received.

Linda was in Tucson, Arizona when news reached her that the Republican leader, Liam Lynch had been killed in action on 10 April 1923. She played down the effect of his death in an interview with the *Tucson Citizen*.

'The moment always finds the man and we have many men left alive who are every bit as good to take the place of the slain soldier. In guerilla warfare there is never any leader of supreme power in the field. The commanding officer of the moment is the man in power and when he is captured or killed there are always men quite as competent to step into his place. Liam Lynch was a member of the military staff, and in no way the figurehead the dispatches have painted him. His loss is in no way significant, except in a purely sentimental way among us who knew him personally and loved him. There is only one leader in our cause and that is de Valera.'[28]

It is interesting that Linda retained an article written in a San Antonio newspaper, which saw the death of Liam Lynch, a fanatic in the opinion of the reporter, as an opportunity for peace in Ireland:

> 'There will be a greater chance for peace now with Lynch vanished from the scene. As the 'republican' chief of staff he guided operations against Free State troops throughout the country. Towards the end he could not have had more than two or three thousand followers altogether, and only a few hundred in any one place... ... de Valera's one prominent fighter still at liberty is Dan Breen. If he is killed or captured, de Valera will have a hard time prolonging the conflict.'[29]

The article went on to say that the destruction of railway bridges and private property by republicans had turned the majority of the people against them.

Early in March 1923 Linda learned of the death of her cousin Tommy Goff who was shot by Free State soldiers at Beltra, Co. Sligo on 15 February. Goff's mother, Julia Clarke, was Linda's first cousin. His father, a native of Roscommon was a member of the R.I.C. Tommy Goff joined the British army and saw action in France in the Royal Flying Corps during the first World War. He became involved in the training of the Volunteers in the Dromard area during the War of Independence.[30]

One of the highlights of the tour for Linda and Kathleen Boland was the garden party given by Mrs. Joseph P Phelan at her 'sumptuous home', 1246, Highland Avenue, Fall River, Massachusetts on Saturday, 23 June 1923. Despite the inclement weather over 300 guests turned up. The American flag and the Irish tricolour were positioned at the front of the house and 'at intervals along the hedge of greenery that delineated the front boundary of the estate were placed numerous miniature flags of both nations.' Ices and cakes were sold from a booth on the lawn and young women dressed in white with sashes of green, white and orange served salads and tea in the house. Linda wore a 'stunning gown of emerald green, green stockings and green slippers. On her right shoulder and left breast were pinned Tara brooches and the green, brown and grey embroidery on her sleeves symbolized the plaid pattern costume worn by her family's clan.' Kathleen wore an afternoon frock of grey embroidered crepe de chine while the hostess Mrs. Phelan had chosen an imported French gown of printed crepe.

More than 200 whist tables had been arranged on the lawn but due to a rain shower these had to be removed and the whist programme was not proceeded with. Instead the prizes for the card game were raffled off. The speeches were delivered from the rear terrace of the house with the guests seated in a series of semi-circles on the lawn. Linda labelled the Free State the 'Freak State' and she repeated a theme she had used in many of her previous speeches, namely the false result of the June 1922 general election: a result, she claimed, that would have been different had not many republicans been disenfranchised because they were in prison. Many others, who were on the run, found it impossible to exercise their vote. In appealing directly for funds she instanced the case of Mrs. Whelan whose son was executed in 1920 and who 'three weeks ago left her home to bid goodbye to her second and last son who was also to be executed. The woman is old. She has no means of support. Her husband is dead. Her sons are now dead. All her loved ones are dead: all died fighting for what they thought was right. She needs help if ever anyone needed help. Think of your own mother in this situation. Give'[31]

Towards the end of 1923, Kathleen Brady, a native of Belfast and Rev Michael O'Flanagan joined Linda and

Kathleen Boland in addressing meetings. Fr. O'Flanagan's first public appearance was in Newark, New Jersey and he also spoke in the Memorial Hall, Cincinnati where he declared that Ireland was fighting the same war against England that the thirteen colonies fought in 1776.[32] A resolution was adopted at this meeting calling on the President of the United States ... to use the influence of the government in obtaining the release of all Irish political prisoners. In Providence, Rhode Island, in October, Miss Brady called for the release of Éamon de Valera who had been imprisoned the previous August. She told the audience: 'Free Staters are trying to place the cause of the recent civil war on the shoulders of de Valera and in order to do this they have accused him of breaking the pact of May, 1922. Arthur Griffith worked against this pact. Michael Collins signed the pact and then after he had gone to England in connection with the Treaty, returned to Ireland and repudiated it.' The pact referred to was an electoral agreement between de Valera and Collins whereby candidates from the pro- and anti-treaty parties would contest forthcoming elections on the same panel under the Sinn Féin banner. Under pressure from the British government, who deemed the pact to be in contravention of the Treaty, Collins disclaimed it.

A newspaper report of a republican meeting in the Moose Hall, Philadelphia, on 22 October 1923, claimed that the $15,000 donated was 'bullet money.' Linda wrote to the editor stating that she resented the implication that the money was collected under false pretences. 'The money is solely and entirely used for relief purposes and your statement may be the cause of the Free State Government confiscating money which is to provide food for the women and children starving in Ireland.' Speakers at this meeting which was chaired by Luke Dillon, president of the Irish-American Club included Rev. Michael O'Flanagan, Kathleen Brady, Kathleen Boland and Linda. Among the subscriptions were; $1000 from the Council of America Club, $2000 from two companies of the Irish

Republican Volunteers, and $1000 from the Irish-American club. On February 10, 1924 Linda was the principal speaker at a meeting chaired by Thomas J. Monaghan in Carbondale, Pennsylvania. The other speakers were Edward Harty who had just returned from a fact-finding visit to Ireland and James E.Loftus of Olyphant an authority on Irish affairs.[33]

For the latter part of her stay in America Linda was given overall responsibility for the correspondence relating to the Dependents Fund. In fulfilling this role she worked out of the Park Avenue Hotel in New York. On her return to Ireland she was replaced by J. J. O Kelly T.D. By this time other republican advocates had arrived in the States. These included Máire Comerford, Mrs Tom Clarke, Mrs. Margaret Pearse and Seán Moylan.

Despite the gruelling schedule, involving long tedious train journeys, occasional small meetings and the pressure of meeting deadlines, Linda and Kathleen seemed to have enjoyed the tour. Linda told Annie Smithson that 'America is a wonderful country and I love it, and the American people are with us heart and soul. They sympathise with us in our sufferings and they also approve of this stand we are making for freedom and independence.'[34] For Hanna Sheehy Skeffington it was less appealing perhaps. (Incidentally, Kathleen, in her diary, always refers to Hanna as Mrs. Skeffington whereas the christian name is used in Linda's case). The women's leisure time was spent shopping, going to the cinema and visiting friends. Parties in hotels and private houses were frequent. Kathleen seems to have taken to ice cream which apparently was new to her. On the other hand Linda found the chewing of gum especially by young girls, disgusting![35] When the women arrived in a city or town it was customary for a host family such as the Castellinis in Cincinnati to show them the sights. For example they visited Thompson Park on the Harding Trail and went down the Anaconda mine in Montana. It was in Montana that they saw 'a fully fledged cowboy on a horse and dressed in cowboy attire.'

California in particular held many attractions for them. Kathleen writes of enjoying life in the sunshine in the Santa Clara Valley and in the area around Sonoma. She was struck by the beauty of the Pacific on reaching San Jose. In Hollywood, Los Angeles she saw the film *The Hunchback of Notre Dame* in the making while in Chinatown, San Francisco she ate chop suey possibly for the first time. The following extract from her diary details her activities around Christmas 1922 in Westfield, Massachusetts when there was a break from the round of meetings.

> 22 December—Shopped for Mrs. Skeffington and got a bag, set of pearls, scent spray and a $5 bill from Miss Leahy and Miss Flynn.
>
> 23 December—Up at 7 o'clock, at station to Westfield at four minutes past eight—rush to get seat—arrived in Westfield via Springfield at 1.30—had lunch in Kimbal Hotel and went to Confession—went to Mrs. and Mary Hearn and were very kindly received – rested.
>
> 24 Sunday—went to Xmas Eve Mass and to Midnight Mass and Communion—went back and had supper. We went to Polish church to Midnight Mass.
>
> 25th Monday—Mass and on Xmas morning had a wonderful gift from Mrs. and Mr. Hearn and Mary-- 10 dollars in gold and gloves, laces, pins and chocolate—dinner in Hearns. We said rosary nightly.
>
> 26th Saw doctor—went to Westfield to pictures.
>
> 27th Went to Springfield to pictures.
>
> 28th Snowed all day—the lovely picture it is in this wonderful place.
>
> 29th The sunshine on the snow and the sleighs, like a picture card. The fun we had sleighing and we are to leave on Saturday

30th Back in New York 9.30—long tiresome trip.[36]

Mrs. Sara Quinn Hill, secretary of the Patrick Henry Council of the A.A.R.I.R. in Los Angeles left the following pen picture of Linda:

'I met Nurse Kearns on the day of her departure and together we lunched at a little café near her stopping place. It was during this short time that I came to realise the marvelous strength of character, and calm, fearless nature of this Irish girl patriot. Miss Kearns speaks in a softly modulated tone of voice, but one can glean the masterful and unflinching courage behind every accent. I accompanied her while she finished a bit of last minute shopping. She bought knitting needles to make sweaters for the soldiers on her railroad journeys. As we parted she leaned forward and kissed me. My own eyes filled with tears as I watched the straight, slender figure disappear in the crowd. Maybe I would never see big, dark-eyed, handsome Nurse Linda Kearns in California again. But I would carry forever the memory of one of the bravest daughters of the Irish Republic-truly an Irish soldier girl.'[37]

The effect of the tour on the Irish in America was summed up by a supporter in New Orleans:

'They came one evening –just two girls with laughing brown eyes and now they have gone and we are desolate. We heard and read of these Irishwomen but we did not realise what their visit would mean to us. If we thought of them at all apart from their mission we imagined them older women hardened by suffering and imprisonment. Instead two Irish colleens came to us for one week and brought us laughter, sunshine and tears. For that one week we who left Ireland many years ago and others who never saw it were there in spirit. We were in Ireland and we now have a clearer vision of the suffering and courage of these Irishwomen. They left us and we miss them; crowds went to the depot to get one last glimpse of them and have a last handshake; a porter was kept busy carrying boxes of candies, flowers, parcels of keepsakes to their compartment; we all cried, some openly, some surreptitiously. One young man just here from Ireland a few months would not lift his head lest we saw his tears. They are gone and they left behind a splendid impression. They have made us proud of our Irish blood and thankful for the privilege of meeting and knowing Linda Kearns and Kathleen Boland.'[38]

The overall success of this tour[39] was the result of a number of factors, in particular the role of the American Association for the Recognition of The Irish Republic (A.A.R.I.R) which had been launched by Éamonn De Valera in November, 1920, at Washington. Many of the women's meetings in cities all over the U.S. were held under the auspices of this organisation. Occasionally different councils of the A.A.R.I.R. vied with one another in their efforts to ensure a good turnout and a worthwhile collection when the women arrived in a venue to deliver their speeches. It is important to remember also that Linda and her friends benefitted from the groundwork laid by a host of other activists who had visited America previously, for example, Seán MacDiarmada, Mary MacSwiney, and especially Harry Boland. Harry's friend, the veteran Fenian, Luke Dillon welcomed the women to Philadelphia. However there is no reference to Joseph McGarrity, perhaps the most influential of all the American supporters, in the diary of Kathleen Boland. Another major factor which contributed to the success of the tour was the Catholic Church network involving priests, nuns and occasionally bishops. In Kathleen's account there are frequent references to priests who attended meetings and sometimes spoke at them. These priests were also generous in their hospitality and contributions. It was customary for Linda and Kathleen to visit convents where they felt at home and where they received donations and gifts. The third factor was the ability and willingness of Irish-American women to convene meetings, provide accommodation and organise social activities for the speakers. A prominent organisation in this regard was the Ladies Auxiliary of Clan na Gael. Another interesting feature of this tour is the interest shown by non-Irish-American organisations. We find for example that Linda, Hanna and Kathleen were the dinner guests of the President of the Illinois League of Women Voters on one occasion when they were in Chicago.

Linda returned to Ireland in the spring of 1924. One of her first public engagements was in Sligo on Easter Sunday when she took part in a huge demonstration to commemorate the eight anniversary of the Rising and also to celebrate the recent release of political prisoners. Her friend, Michael Nevin, now mayor, presided and also present were Mrs Tom Clarke and local republicans including D.A. Mulcahy. Nevin, in the course of his speech, referred to the dismissal of the Browne family from the local gas works because of their republican leanings. He also read a letter from Mary MacSwiney on this particular issue. Linda received a tremendous ovation when she was introduced to the crowd. Speaking from the steps of the Town Hall, she gave an account of her experiences in America and she also highlighted the case of the Brownes whose brother was 'doing great work' in America.[40]

A few weeks later she was in Limerick canvassing for Tadhg Crowley, who was contesting a bye-election on behalf of Sinn Féin. Here she was joined by Madame Markievicz, Hanna Sheehy-Skeffington, Robert Brennan and Seán T. O Kelly. Crowley lost the election but the Free State candidate's majority was cut by 19,000 votes. [41]

In the autumn of 1924 Linda and Kathleen Maloney (née Barry), a sister of Kevin Barry sailed to Australia[42] and spent almost five months on a fund-raising tour. Between them they addressed over fifty meetings in Queensland, New South Wales and Victoria. They carried with them letters from Éamon De Valera and from the Reconstruction Committee of the Irish Republican Prisoners' Dependents Fund (I.R.P.D.F.). The letter of the Reconstruction Committee, dated 6 September, 1924 was signed by the honorary treasurers, Kathleen Clarke and Mrs. Kean and by the chairman, Art Ó Conchubair.[43] It stated that the committee was directing its efforts

> 'towards restoring to civilian occupation men and women on the Republican side who by direct participation in the war of adhesion to the Republican cause, lost opportunities of education or training to fit them for permanent, productive effort or found their means of living destroyed. These men and women gave of their best to achieve independence for Ireland. The reward offered them by those who at present control the resources of the country is emigration or starvation.'

The letter went on to refer to the *Military Pensions Act* which was passed the previous month and which debarred anti-Treaty soldiers from receiving pensions. Whereas this letter emphasised the humanitarian object of the proposed tour, de Valera's missive was much more political in tone. Dated 1, September 1924 it was headed Dáil Éireann, Oifig an Uachtaráin, Báile Átha Cliath. (de Valera had been released from prison the previous July).[44]

TO EVERY FRIEND OF THE IRISH REPUBLIC IN AUSTRALIA GREETINGS.

The continued support which our friends in Australia have given the cause of the Republic in the recent trying years has been of inestimable value in enabling us to carry on the struggle for freedom. That struggle is now entered on its final stage and it remains for those who have continued steadfast to intensify their efforts, that the position held prior to December 6th 1921 may be restored in the shortest time. Events are moving rapidly in our favour; our people at home are reawakened; our people abroad are equally alive to the possibilities of the next few months. Organisation and coordination of effort at home and abroad are immediate and pressing duties so that any opportunity may not be missed.

The tone of this tour was much different from that of

America. The emphasis this time was very much on the extreme distress of republicans and their families. The dissension and bitterness of the recent Civil War were not referred to, at least in public. In fact Linda and other speakers were at pains to reassure audiences that 'the mission was one of pure charity and that no one need have any fear of compromising his national, political or religious creed. Their concern was to show and prove that charity existed among the people here for those in distress in the home of the race to which most of them belonged.'[45] There was another noticeable difference between the American and Australian tours in that Linda and Kathy Barry did a lot of organisational work, arranging meetings, contacting Irish groups and visiting schools whereas in 1922-23, the A.A.I.R.R. in particular did a great deal of the groundwork.[46] However it must be said that, on this second tour for Linda, once the preparatory work was done the Irish community was eager to give its support. For example in Brisbane, the Hibernian Society through the president, J.A. Herbert and the secretary Peter Scott were quick to notify the various branches of their society of the mission of the two women by sending the following letter to *The Catholic Press*.

> 'There are in Brisbane today two ladies, Kathleen Barry and Linda Kearns soliciting subscriptions for the relief of distress in Ireland. A strong committee has been formed in Brisbane with His Grace, Archbishop Duhig as patron. It is the wish of your executive that the appeal should be successful and that Queensland should be foremost in assisting the suffering and the poor in Ireland. Each and everyone of us can help by subscribing, by asking friends and sympathisers to help and by assisting the delegates to arrange meetings in Brisbane and the other cities which they may visit. Charity knows no creed or nationality, and we confidently appeal to you to assist in making the delegation a great financial success.'[47]

One of the first meetings took place in Melbourne on 16 November where Archbishop Mannix was the principal speaker. A huge crowd heard him open the proceedings as follows:

'I have just been reminded in the words of Miss Kearns that I am here at the call of the blood...I am here because my kith and kin are suffering in the homeland. But I come here all the more readily, because those who are now suffering in Ireland are those who have never lowered their flag of Ireland or acknowledged any allegiance to any foreign power...British propaganda has a long hand and we were assured here and some who should have known better accepted the assurance that Ireland's trouble was happily ended, when the so-called Treaty was signed. We were told with growing confidence that not 20%, nor 10%, not even 2% of the Irish people would reject the London agreement, that President de Valera could scarcely get his nomination paper filled in Co. Clare, his own constituency; that the republicans were just a few crazy scatter-brained Irish boys and a few hysterical Irish women. This afternoon you have two of the hysterical Irish women. You can make a good guess at what the scatter brained Irish boys are like... Ah! We are all wiser now. The scales fell from our eyes, when, in spite of what seemed insuperable difficulties forty four Republicans were returned at the last election to the Dáil to which they had too much consistency and self-respect to enter. I expect before long to see the Republican party in a perfectly constitutional way prove their right at the ballot box to govern Ireland. Meanwhile we must be patient even with those who have differed from us; and patience will bring its reward. Don't trust those British propagandist papers which tell you with crocodile tears that religion is dead or dying in Ireland. Catholic Ireland is at heart as sound and loyal as ever ... and Catholic Ireland, moreover, is prepared to be as fair and as tolerant as she has always been to non-Catholic Irishmen. For myself, I look forward to a speedy healing of the wounds, political and religious, from which Ireland has been recently suffering. I look forward to a free and undivided Ireland in which those who have differed and even fought in civil strife can bury the terrible past and work for their common motherland. I wish to thank you all for the enthusiastic welcome which you have given to our distinguished visitors. This great meeting will I trust give them heart and cheer in the arduous work which they have come to do in Australia. I thank you also for the generous response which you have made to their appeal. I hope it is a good omen for the success of the appeal throughout the Commonwealth.[48]

Archbishop Duhig contributed £20 to the fund. The committee president was M.J. Kirwan, Assistant Home Secretary in Queensland with Alderman P.A. McLachlin and Peter Gaffney, treasurers and Peter Scott, secretary. Linda and Kathy spoke in the Exhibition Hall on 16 January. However because of the huge distances to be covered, they decided to divide the work between them. They were given 'all lines' railway passes on the authority of Theodore the Queensland premier who received them in his office after the meeting in Exhibition Hall. Other prominent politicians who lent their support included the Attorney-General, Mr. Mullan and the Minister for Agriculture Mr. McCormack. McCormack wrote to the Brisbane committee: 'In response to the appeal of Miss Barry and Miss Kearns for help in relieving distress in Ireland, I am forwarding herewith my cheque for £5. I sincerely trust that the appeal will meet with generous support.'[49]

Kathy Barry concentrated her efforts mostly in Northern Queensland, speaking in Rockhampton, Mount Morgan, Mackay, Townsville, Innisfail and Cairns. On 11 February she addressed a meeting in Ipswich organised by the local Relief Committee under the chairmanship of Monsignor Byrne. Earlier in the day she was introduced to the railway workers by Tim Moroney of the Australian Railway Union. Addressing individual groups was a feature of this tour. Schools were also visited by the two women.

Linda spoke in Bundaberg, Beaudesert, Maryborough, Toowomba Warwick and Gympie. At the meeting in the Olympia Theatre in Gympie, 28 January 1925, she said that the hardship following a long period of strife in Ireland was compounded by the exceptionally wet weather of the previous two years resulting in poor harvests. Seed potatoes were very scarce and 'it was for the purpose of providing the farmers with assistance in that direction and to help others in various callings in life who needed financial help, that their mission to Australia had been undertaken. With regard to helping those in distress, they should not consider whether they deserved it, but think of all the suffering and starvation that existed and needed relief.' Mr Jer Carey proposed that a subscription list be opened in Gympie and that it be kept open until 7 February. He felt he could move the resolution 'on the broad platform of common charity.' The motion was seconded by Mr D. Mulcahy and passed unanimously. £110 was subscribed at the meeting. Fr. O'Flynn contributed £20, the largest subscription.[50]

On 2 February Linda addressed the staff and students of the Christian Brothers High School in Maryborough where she was presented with *The Songs of a Sentimental Bloke* by the Australian poet and journalist, C.J.Dennis (1876-1938).[51] Dennis had been educated at the Christian Brothers' College in Adelaide. Linda also had in her possession another book by Dennis, *The Moods of Ginger Mick*, which she may have acquired on this tour.

According to a Brisbane newspaper[52] the Queensland campaign would close with a second meeting in the Exhibition Hall, on 12 February presided over by Archbishop Duhig and attended by Fr. O'Flynn, 'the silver-tongued orator of Gympie' and other Catholic clergy.

'A Grand Farewell Concert will be tendered the delegates by the pupils of the catholic schools, church choirs and leading artists. The price to all parts of the hall has been fixed at one shilling with children 6d. The occasion will be the last lovers of Ireland and admirers of heroic girlhood in Kathleen Barry and Linda Kearns will have of helping the needy and distressed of Ireland to seek succour for whom the delegates have come 12,000 miles to Australia.'

A newspaper reporter described Linda as 'a brunette, with a typically Irish face expressive of her calling– a nurse by profession.' When asked her impression of Australia and Queensland, 'her eyes sparkled with delight as she answered that she loved Australia, the Australian, Queensland and the Queenslander with whom she found herself immediately at home so to speak. Although the people of America were good, kind and responsive, the Queenslanders were even more kindly disposed.'[53]

Linda and Kathy were given a civic reception in Sydney. A large audience assembled in the Town Hall when the Lord Mayor, Alderman Stokes welcomed them to the city and expressed the hope that the success of the mission in Queensland and Victoria would be repeated in New South Wales. Replying Kathy said that there a lot of distress in Ireland apart from that being experienced by released political prisoners and their families and the mission to Australia was an effort to prevent starvation and the need to emigrate. It was therefore in no way political. The welcome extended to Linda and Kathy came under attack from sections of the Tory press in Sydney when it was discovered that the toast to King George V had not been delivered at the civic reception. The Federal government was requested to get involved but in the event no action was taken.[54]

Archbishop Mannix attended a concert for the Irish Relief Fund organised by the Irish Pipers' Association in the Cathedral Hall, Fitzroy. Mannix told the audience that the signing of the Treaty was one of the tragedies of Irish history. 'When it was signed every instrument of British propaganda said that Ireland had got a settlement of which she could be proud. I have never trusted British propaganda. Ireland has not accepted the Treaty and never will.' Linda told the meeting that £2000 had been raised in Victoria and £1,500 had already been cabled to

Ireland. The balance would be sent during the week.[55]

In a newspaper interview after returning to Ireland Kathleen Barry admitted that 'as was only to be expected we found things difficult at first.' The Irish-Australians had become very disillusioned by the Treaty and the Civil War and 'interest in the movement was almost killed.' Consequently 'the first business of the mission was in a word, spadework.' She acknowledged that the role of the Catholic papers in Sydney, Melbourne and Brisbane had been vital for the success of the mission. 'Without them we should have had terrible difficulties.' Another publication which she singled out for particular mention was the *Irish Nation*, a monthly produced in Melbourne by 'a few staunch republicans.' She also paid tribute to the three archbishops, Sheehan, Duhig and especially Mannix, who was 'a host in himself.' Political support was strongest in Queensland where the premier, Theodore and a number of ministers were open in their backing of the mission. Theodore's wife was personally responsible for raising £100. The final figure for the amount raised was expected to reach £8,000 of which £6,000 had already been distributed. Kathleen concluded: 'I have seen reports of the cases dealt with and while it is cheering to see so much done for £6,000, it is saddening to think how much more could be done for £60,000. However we have done our best and Irish-Australia did well for us.'[56]

Dr Mannix visited Ireland in the summer of 1925 and was given tremendous receptions in all the centres in which he spoke. His pending arrival had been reported widely in the press. At the civic reception in Dublin, Linda was among de Valera's party. Charlotte Despard and Maud Gonne McBride were also invited by de Valera.[57]

Chapter Seven
Fianna Fail

At the Sinn Fein Ard-Fheis of March 1926, Éamon de Valera proposed that the Sinn Fein party should consider entering Dáil Éireann provided that the oath of allegiance was removed and when that was achieved it became 'a question not of principle but of policy whether or not republican representatives should attend these assemblies'.[1] He failed by a narrow margin to win over the delegates and a few weeks later he formally launched a new party, Fianna Fáil. The launch which was presided over by Madame Markievicz took place in the La Scala Theatre in Prince's Street, Dublin on 16 May.[2] De Valera invoked memories of 1916 by quoting James Connolly: 'Ireland, as distinct from her people, is nothing to me'. Although *An Phoblacht* gave the event sparse coverage, confining itself to a single paragraph its tone was favourable; 'the scenes at La Scala Theatre on Sunday with the great building thronged to the doors and the streets outside filled with masses of people unable to get in has come as nasty shock to the Free State Party managers'.[3]

Linda was one of six women voted onto the first executive of the new party. The others were; Hanna Sheehy Skeffington, Kathleen Clarke, Madame Markievicz, Margaret Pearse and Dorothy Macardle. With the exception of Dorothy all of them were in some way associated with the 1916 Rising. None of them however became part of the decision making of the party. This was reserved for Gerry Boland, Seán Lemass and a few more close associates of de Valera.[4]

Dorothy Macardle was Linda's closest friend although it is unknown when their friendship began. She was a frequent visitor to Linda's home 29 Gardiner Place and on one occasion at least she was given nursing care there during a bout of illness.[5] Family sources tell of Linda and Dorothy confiding in each other especially when women's issues became contentious in the 1930s.[6] Dorothy was born into a unionist family, the Macardles who were well-known brewers in Dundalk, Co. Louth. Her father was Sir Thomas Macardle KBE, DL. She espoused the cause of Republicanism in the War of Independence and took the anti-Treaty side in the Civil War during which she was twice imprisoned. When the Catholic Hierarchy excommunicated all republicans she publicly renounced her religion. After the *Irish Press* was founded Dorothy became its drama critic. She also attended sessions of the League of Nations for the paper when de Valera was president in 1938. During the Second World War she worked on behalf of refugee children and in 1951 she was appointed president of the Irish Association of Civil Liberties. A prolific writer, she is the author of several novels, short stories and histories, one of which *The Irish Republic* is essential reading for a study of the 1916-1923 period. This work which was published in 1937 was written at the request of de Valera who also wrote the preface. Considering that she was one of the leading champions of women's rights her failure to give due recognition in this monumental work to the influence exerted by Mary MacSwiney, Hanna Sheehy Skeffington, Kathleen Clarke and others is surprising. Linda, who is listed as one of the sources in the acknowledgements, is referred to twice in the book. The first describes her capture in Sligo and the second mentions her role in the events surrounding the death of Cathal Brugha. Dorothy Macardle died in 1958.[7]

A few months after the founding of Fianna Fáil, de Valera wrote letters to Linda, Madame Markievicz, Hannah Sheehy Skeffington, Seán T Ó Ceallaigh, Gerry Boland and Seán Lemass requesting them to set up a relief committee to oversee the distribution of a donation of £120 which had been sent by the Irish National Association of Australia. Linda replied on headed notepaper that she would 'be glad to act on a relief committee and do what I can to help'. From time to time this fund was augmented by other subscriptions especially from America. De Valera himself, who is referred to as the 'Chief' in correspondence relating to this committee, gave a personal donation of £15. Meetings of this committee were minuted by Kathleen O'Connell, de Valera's secretary and Seán T Ó Ceallaigh was appointed treasurer. The fund was dispensed in amounts usually not above £10 and this sum could be given in instalments. This was done in the case of Mrs. Mainwaring, a patient in Kathleen Lynn's convalescent home, St. Ultans. Linda is recorded as giving £10 to Mrs. Mary Benson of Ballisodare, Co. Sligo. It is unclear how the committee came to a decision as to who should benefit. It may be that that the beneficiaries were relatives of victims of the Troubles.[8]

Linda was a member of the Fianna Fáil executive up to the time of her death though for long periods particularly in the 1940s she did not attend meetings. These absences certainly occurred during her own hospitalisation for a mastectomy and during her daughter's illness in 1941 but they may be explained also by a waning of her enthusiasm for Fianna Fáil especially with the emergence of Clann na Poblachta though she did not become a member of this new party. However if she was unhappy with the direction taken by Fianna Fáil as for example in regard to the 1937 constitution there is no evidence of any protest from her similar to that of Kathleen Clarke who eventually left the party.[9] Her involvement in several other organisations would also have had a bearing on the time she could devote to meetings. Another possible cause of disillusionment on her part was her failure to be elected to the Senate in 1943 when she felt let down by at least one party colleague who had promised his support.[10] Whatever the reasons, between 1944 and 1950 she was almost continually absent although she usually turned up for the first meeting after the annual Ard-Fheis. The last meeting she attended was in July 1950 almost a full year before she died. It is interesting to note that by this time she and Margaret Pearse were the only women on the executive.

The National Executive covered a wide range of issues and topics ranging from the organisation of the Ard-Fheis to the use of the bar in Leinster House by persons who were not members of the Oireachtas! Particular attention was paid to the vetting and selection of candidates for elections. An important decision in this regard was taken at a special meeting, chaired by de Valera in May 1937 when the following motion was passed:

The National Executive hereby takes power to add a name or names to the Panel of Candidates to be nominated at the General Election for any constituency, wherein it appears to it that such action is essential to strengthen the panel, to serve the best interests of the organisation and to secure a maximum vote at the polls.[11]

The annual national collection was organised by the executive who kept a close eye on the amount of money collected and cumainn were liable to censure if the figure realised did not come up to expectations. In regard to the share out of the takings, a decision was taken in February 1937 that two thirds of the sum collected would go to the national organisation with the constituency retaining the remainder.

It is difficult to assess Linda's influence at this level of the Fianna Fáil organisation especially since the minutes for the first nine years of the executive are either lost or unavailable. At the 1937 April meeting, she spoke at length on four issues. The first was what she called 'the renovation of emblems of the British in institutions under Government control such as at the Curragh.' She then raised the question of the presence of British soldiers in Dublin and other towns who were alleged to be distributing recruiting forms for the British army and also travel vouchers. Her next topic concerned 'the use of the High Commissioner's office in London for the sale of tickets at half price for accommodation at the coronation ceremony'. Finally she objected to the circulation in Ireland of a British periodical called *The Wizard*. The Executive decided to bring these issues to the attention of the relevant government ministers.[12] Later in the same year Linda stated at a meeting that the showing of a certain film, which she did not name, in Dublin 'would lead to breaches of the peace if it were allowed to be further circulated'.[13] The Minister for Justice responding later said that he had no power to prohibit circulation.[14] The following year Linda was elected a senator on the Industrial and Commercial Panel on the nomination of the Women's Industrial Development Association. *(see Chapter 11)*

The war years presented particular problems some of which were widely discussed by the executive. One of these was the decision made by certain republican prisoners to go on hunger strike after the passing of *The Offences against the State Act* in June 1939. The Government refused to bow to requests to release them. At a meeting at the end of 1939 Linda asked that this decision be rescinded in the case of one particular prisoner, Patrick McGrath who was physically handicapped. He had been prominent in the War of Independence. McGrath was released but the following August he was executed for his part in the murder of two detectives.[15] It is clear from the tone of the meetings that there was a certain amount of sympathy for political prisoners on the part of some members including Linda. Back at the end of 1936 a motion was proposed that 'owing to the near approach of Christmas we should be glad if the Executive Council would give consideration to the question of the release of political prisoners'. However this particular motion was withdrawn after a lengthy discussion. Another indication of the concern of some members for the political prisoners was a request to the Minister for Defence Gerry Boland at the meeting of 8 April 1940 to furnish information on 'the genesis of the hungerstrike and the conditions of the strikers'.

Another matter which provoked a great deal of comment was a fundraising drive in some parts of the Free State (particularly in Co. Monaghan), to aid the production of British aircraft. Apparently contributions were being made by both firms and individuals. When questioned, Gerry Boland said that it was not possible 'to subject all activities of this nature to control'.[16]

Early in 1941 Frank Sherwin complained that the air-raid shelters in Dublin were totally inadequate. He called for underground shelters which could be used in the development of a transport system at the conclusion of the war.[17]

The executive frequently discussed issues raised by individual cumainn or constituency organisations. Among these was a call in December 1938 from the Michael Mallin cumann of Dublin South for the return of the remains of Roger Casement to Ireland.[18] In January 1939 a request from Sandyford cumann to abolish hanging[19] as a capital punishment was referred to the Minister for Justice as was the question of flogging in 1941.[20]

The executive devoted almost an entire meeting to a discussion on the *County Management Bill 1940*.[21] A proposal that 'the county manager and his staff shall be completely subject to the control and direction of the county council' was defeated. Another management issue: that of the National College of Art was brought up in a motion in the name of Bernard Butler in January 1942. He proposed that 'the National Executive recommend to the Department of Education that the National College of Art should be directed and staffed by Irish nationals and in furtherance of this recommendation, that all future appointments to the National College of Art should be confined to Irish nationals'. Discussion on this motion was deferred.[22]

The subject of partition was very much to the fore at meetings from late 1938 to mid 1940. During this period the role of the government was queried on a number of occasions and several proposals were put forward with the objective of strengthening anti-partition sentiment not only in Ireland but also in England. At the 1938 October special meeting a motion in four parts was put forward:

1. To cooperate with the six county anti-partition movement in organising anti-partition demonstrations in that area.
2. To set up a sub-committee to consider the organisation of public opinion in England on the question of partition.
3. That the question of a suitable pamphlet be referred to the publicity committee.
4. That an anti-partition meeting be held in Dublin on 23 October.[23]

A sub-committee was indeed set up by the executive but the public demonstration to be held in Dublin was deferred due to the fact that de Valera's presence could not be guaranteed since he was proposing to visit the United States. Other measures taken regarding the partition question included the decisions to give £100 to the Liverpool anti-partition organisation and to send P.J. Little T.D. to England to investigate the possibility of establishing an anti-partition league in London. De Valera effectively rounded off the partition debate when at the 1940 July meeting he 'explained the line of policy which the government had decided to follow'. The minutes do not record what this policy was.[24]

In 1948 Fianna Fáil were out power for the first time in sixteen years after the general election of that year when their number of seats dropped from seventy six to sixty eight. The national executive reacted with a series of measures designed to recover lost ground. Seán McEntee was appointed head of a committee to investigate the party's failure in certain Dublin City constituencies and in Dún Laoghaire-Rathdown. Erskine Childers was given the role of publicity officer, on a part time basis, at £350 per annum. Then early in 1949, 60,000 leaflets promoting the party were distributed nationwide. A proposal of Joe Groome to make £2,000 available for 'publicity and propaganda purposes' entailing a general campaign of meetings throughout the country and the publication of party literature was withdrawn after discussion at a meeting in July 1948.[25]

The 1937 Constitution which seemed to many women a far cry from the sentiments expressed in the 1916 proclamation, was discussed on a number of occasion by the executive but mostly in the context of Mrs. Kathleen Clarke's opposition to it. There is no record in the minutes of any protest being registered by Linda and indeed it would appear that Mrs. Clarke's was the only dissenting voice. Linda was present at three meetings when Mrs. Clarke was criticised especially by Seán O'Donovan who proposed the motion 'that this executive considers that support for the constitution at the recent plebiscite was an obligation on all members of the Fianna Fáil organisation and party'. It is clear that that there was some sympathy for Mrs. Clarke if not for her stance when O'Donovan was asked to withdraw his motion and on his refusing to do so the meeting bypassed the issue by passing another motion 'to proceed to the next business'.[26] Indeed the members had already agreed, on foot of a query of Mrs. Clarke, 'that the free expression of opinion on non-party matters by members of the organisation was not contrary to rule'.[27]

Mrs. Clarke came under attack from her own cumann named after her husband, which she herself had established, and of which she was chairperson. The secretary of the cumann Mr. E. Timmons wrote to the executive regarding her 'attitude to Bunreacht na hÉireann'. A similar letter was sent by the secretary of the North Dock cumann Mr. G. Hughes. Again the response of the executive was conciliatory. A motion in the names of Gerry Boland and Padraic Ó Máille 'that Messrs Timmons and Hughes be informed that the executive had considered this matter on previous occasions and it was decided that no action be taken' was carried.[28] Mrs. Clarke who became Lord Mayor of Dublin in 1940, resigned from Fianna Fáil three years later.

There can be little doubt that Linda had at least misgivings about some aspects of the 1937 constitution. Her friend Dorothy Macardle certainly had and said in the aftermath of its acceptance that she had wasted seven years in the writing of her book *The Irish Republic*.[29] But Linda does not appear to have said anything publicly in protest much less gone down the road taken by Kathleen Clarke. In answer to a query on this subject her nephew said that her unswerving loyalty to and admiration for de Valera kept her firmly within the Fianna Fáil party. It is worth recording also that she was on very friendly terms with de Valera and his family.[30] Another reason which may have influenced her was the fact that it was around this time that the grand scheme of her life i.e. the establishment of a holiday home for nurses was being formulated in her mind and she may have realized that the accomplishment of this ideal might require substantial government assistance.

Chapter Eight
Charles Wilson MacWhinney & Marriage

In September 1929 Linda married Charles Wilson MacWhinney who had been O/C of the Derry Brigade of the I.R.A. during the War of Independence.[1] He had come to Dublin in 1924 after serving a two year prison sentence and resided at first at 3 Gardiner Place, the property of Linda's sister Annie and her husband John Mulligan.[2] It was there that Charles (or Wilson as he was more commonly known in Dublin) and Linda probably met. Charles Wilson MacWhinney who had a Doctorate of Science in engineering, was born on 17 July 1888 to Arthur W. MacWhinney of Draperstown and Bessie Wilson Magill. Arthur was a Clerk of the petty sessions. Bessie was a daughter of Rev Adam Magill Presbyterian minister of Bovevagh, Co. Derry who was ordained in 1843. He married Matilda (Tilly) Susanna, daughter of John Wilson of Fethard, Co. Tipperary in 1845. They had nine children. Bessie, Charles' mother was born in 1850. Her future husband Arthur died in 1893. Bessie, of whom Linda was very fond, died in 1931.

Charles MacWhinney and his mother came to Dublin where she had a house in Appian Way. Charles attended a Boys' school in Clontarf and later went to the Royal University to study engineering. He worked for a time in the Velox works in Liverpool and later in Farnborough in the aeronautical business.[3]

MacWhinney because of his Presbyterian upbringing attracted a lot of attention from both the Loyalist side, to whom he was a traitor and from the Republicans who promoted him as a champion in the mould of former famous Protestant leaders.[4] During the War of Independence he was employed as a teacher of engineering subjects in the Municipal Technical School in Derry and resided at 33 Westland Avenue. While on holidays in the summer of

1921 he was in charge of an I.R.A. camp in the Sperrin Mountains. The R.U.C. suspected that he was one of the main organisers of the attempted rescue of Republican prisoners from Derry Jail, the following December, during which two policemen lost their lives.[5]

MacWhinney first came under police notice when he was convicted of riotous behaviour in Belfast in July 1920 and fined forty shillings. Then on 1 March 1921 he was arrested with William Boyle and Michael McCormack at the corner of Union Street and North Street, Belfast at 10.15 pm. According to the police MacWhinney had in his possession 'a fully detonated No. 5 mills bomb, ready for throwing and number of documents relating to No. 1 Brigade, 3rd Division of the I.R.A.' These documents indicated that he was an instructor in the signalling corps holding the rank of lieutenant. Also in his possession was an notice with the instruction 'you will attend Brigade meeting, St. Mary's Hall, Friday evening.' The three men were prosecuted in the Belfast Custody Court a week later. MacWhinney declared that he was a member of the I.R.A. and refused to recognise the court. He said he was 24—he was in fact ten years older. His statement that he was a labourer was also untrue. 26 Stanhope street was given as his address. He was sentenced to two years' imprisonment with hard labour. McCormack and Boyle were both acquitted for lack of evidence.[6]

MacWhinney was held first in Derry Jail and then on 19 June (1922) he was interned on the prison ship *Argenta* off the coast at Larne.[7] He also spent terms in Larne Workhouse and in Belfast Jail during his two and a half years' incarceration. On the *Argenta* he joined prisoners who had been arrested on 23 May 1922, a night of mass arrests all over the six counties. In all, over three hundred men were rounded up under the *Special Powers Act* of Northern Ireland which had been enacted the previous month.[8] During his short stay on the ship he caused endless problems for the governor A.D. Drysdale. He refused to give personal details– age, next of kin, place of birth-for the official registration form though he appears to have volunteered the information that he was a Presbyterian. Later on, he insisted on the authorities providing religious services for him and the four other Protestant internees.[9] It is unlikely that MacWhinney was totally sincere in his demand: family sources suggest that he was an atheist.[10]

Shortly after the arrest, G.E. Armstrong, M.Sc., principal of the Municipal Technical School, Derry wrote to the Ministry of Education in Belfast stating that 'he had been informed by the local police authorities that Mr MacWhinney was arrested with a view to internment and that no charge was preferred against him.' This communication was followed by a letter to the Minister of Home Affairs, R. Dawson Bates, from J.A. Williams, Secretary, Londonderry County Borough Technical Instruction Committee, with a copy of a resolution passed at a recent meeting of the committee:

> That this committee being informed that their Science Teacher Mr. MacWhinney was arrested by the forces of the Crown on 22nd May last and since detained without charge being formulated against him. We hereby call upon the authorities to formulate their charge against him and place him on his trial or otherwise release him so that the School may not be deprived of the services of a Science teacher. That a copy of this resolution be sent to the Minister for Home Affairs for Northern Ireland and given to the Press.'

In reply Henry Toppin of the Ministry of Home Affairs stated that MacWhinney could 'appeal to the Advisory Committee against his internment and a notice to that effect had been served on him.'[11] Apparently this option was not taken up.

MacWhinney, using the Irish form of his name, Mac Giolla Coinnig, wrote a letter to the Provisional Government in Dublin in July 1922, seeking guidance on the position to be adopted by the internees regarding a couple of important issues. He explained first of all that the internee situation was different than that which obtained prior to the Truce of 1921:

> 'Then the question was a clear issue of loyalty or treachery, and while admittedly a proportion of the men here intend to get out at all costs and at any sacrifice of principle, the majority are prepared to carry on so long as their attitude is of any assistance to their country. To a great many of even the most loyal of the Internees, however, the doubt has come as to whether their sacrifice of liberty is of any value, and I, personally together with a few of my officers would be glad if we could have from you some indication of the policy we are expected to adopt. I have reason to believe that the lead given by myself and my officers will be sufficient for the majority of the men and your suggestion will be treated absolutely in confidence and as unofficial. .... I would suggest you wire to M. O'Kane, SS *Argenta*, Belfast Lough, "Nora getting worse, case hopeless" to indicate we are to recognise the authority of Craig and Co. or accept bail and "Nora slightly better, wait for letter" to tell us to hold on as we are.'[12]

The official decision taken in Dublin stated that 'it was the unanimous opinion of the meeting of the Government that these internees should not give bail.'[13]

On 29 August Charles MacWhinney wrote on behalf of the internees to the governor of the *Argenta*, requesting that he take up the question of parole to attend funerals of relatives with the Northern Ireland government.

> 'It is an inhuman thing to refuse a man permission to visit his home and attend the funeral of say a dead father, mother or wife and apart from the human aspect, in many cases the questions of wills and property might arise. I feel sure that it is not the intention of the Government to treat their prisoners more inhumanly than the Imperial Government did in similar circumstances.'[14]

Around the time of the writing of this letter an inspection of the lower deck of the ship which was now anchored in Larne harbour, revealed that wire screens between the pens occupied by the internees, had been cut leaving holes large enough to allow access from one pen to another. Drysdale, the governor informed the Home Affairs' office in Belfast of this development saying that he feared an attempt at an escape. He suspected that MacWhinney was the ringleader:

> 'Since the *Argenta* was brought to this anchorage a good deal of unrest has been manifested among the internees, and there are several suspicious symtoms pointing to a probable attempt on the part of a number of them to escape, either by an attack on the staff, or by driving a hole through the side of the ship. Every precaution has been adopted by close inspection of the ship and increased vigilance in guarding the internees, but I am of the opinion that it is most important that Internee C. MacWhinney of Westland Avenue, Londonderry, be removed from the ship to a place where he would have less opportunity of instigating the other men to committing serious damage to the staff of the ship. He is I believe, the prime mover in any action which may be contemplated by the internees, and possesses the necessary skill and cunning to carry it through.'[15]

A decision was taken immediately by the Ministry of Home Affairs to transfer MacWhinney to Derry Jail. As to his letter requesting parole for internees in certain cases, it was dismissed on the grounds that 'the dissatisfaction is largely engineered by MacWhinney himself.' On 4 September he was back in Derry and the governor was advised 'to take every precaution to prevent this internee continuing the course of conduct which he appears to have adopted on the ship, and to furnish a report one week after his arrival as to his conduct and demeanour.' In the event MacWhinney's behaviour in his first week in Derry was deemed 'satisfactory' by the governor.[16]

The Technical School authorities wrote again in October 1922 to the Ministry of Home Affairs requesting that MacWhinney be released and allowed to resume his position as teacher. Toppins replied that 'Mr. MacWhinney has not appealed against his internment and the Minister is therefore forced to infer either that he does not recognise the authority of this Government or that he believes that he could not show good grounds against his internment.'[17]

The District Inspector of the R.U.C. in Derry, P. Cahill, advised against releasing MacWhinney: 'This is a clever man of great organising ability which in the event of his release will no doubt be exercised for the advancement of Republicanism...... If released I am strongly of the opinion he will give no guarantee of loyalty to the Northern Government.' Another prominent Derry personality who opposed MacWhinney's release was S.M. Kennedy of the North-West Shirt Factory, 4 Great James Street. He wrote directly to Dawson Bates the Minister for Home Affairs, N.I. with whom he was obviously on friendly terms:

> 'I understand that the Committee of the Technical School here in Derry passed a resolution yesterday, copy of which was to be forwarded to Home Affairs, requesting the release of a teacher of theirs named MacWhinney. This man I think was implicated in the trouble on board the ship, and is back in Derry Jail. The feeling here is very strong against him, in the first place he is supposed to be a Protestant and in the second place his superior education makes him extremely dangerous, so our friends here will be glad if the resolution is ignored. I hear you had a good time in Northern France.'

Dawson Bates wrote back that Kennedy's remarks 'would not be overlooked.'[18]

Early in 1923, Charles MacWhinney wrote to the Ministry of Home Affairs requesting study facilities— writing materials and books– in his cell. In particular he asked for books on aero design, motor design and thermodynamics together with 'books on the mathematics involved, e.g. *Sarby on Mathematics, Low's Applied Mathematics, Gilson's Calculus* etc.' He also requested an

Irish grammar and dictionary. His request was granted although with some reluctance in the case of the books on 'Irish.'

In May, the Ministry of Finance informed Home Affairs that MacWhinney owed a sum of money in income tax in respect of his salary in the Technical School and enquired if there was any likelihood of his release at an early date. The R.U.C. were again consulted and they advised that his case should not be reviewed unless he gave an undertaking to leave Northern Ireland on his release. However, he was not considered 'the type of man who would give any undertaking.'[19]

According to a document of the Inspector General's office, Finger Print Branch of the R.U.C. dated 24 October 1923, MacWhinney was due for release on the 7th of the following month. However District Inspector Lynn of the R.U.C. Belfast D district advised against his release:

> 'While open physical force has been discarded by the Republicans as a policy I think that the release of men like this is still dangerous while Republicanism is active in any shape. This man could be dangerous in Great Britain or Southern Ireland as well as here and I recommend that he be interned and not released.'[20]

In March 1924, MacWhinney was offered a position in the Department of Agriculture in the Free State and the Northern authorities were disposed to releasing him subject to his leaving the Six Counties forever. E.W. Stephenson of the Ministry of Home Affairs commented:

> 'It is improbable that he would accept the conditions of release voluntarily as it would mean the loss of his employment. He could of course be released and served with the order but as he is an intelligent and well educated man he would be likely to follow the example of Cahir Healy.'

The conditions of the release were rejected by Mac Whinney. However he appears to have been an exemplary prisoner as far as the authorities were concerned. There is only one complaint on record from him—one concerning the cleanliness of the food supplied to the internees. According to Dr. M.F. Leslie, the medical officer, there were 'no grounds for the slightest complaint.'[21]

In the last year of his imprisonment MacWhinney had a number of visits from relatives including his brother. His mother, Bessie, who was then residing at 118 Upper Library Street, Belfast wrote to the Ministry of Home Affairs requesting permission to visit for two of her son's first cousins—Mrs Montgomery who resided with her and Miss Liza Bradley of 3 Sydney Street, Belfast. She herself was 'unable to leave the house.' The visit was sanctioned. On other occasions during the year MacWhinney was visited by two other cousins, Miss Catherine (Cassie) McBride of 27 Artillery Street, Belfast and Miss Lizzie Torbitt of Lancashire, England. In June, 1924, James MacWhinney requested permission to see his brother. 'I wish to make application for permission to interview my brother Charles who is at present interned in Larne. As I am leaving for the U.S.A. early in July I would like very much to see him before I leave.' This visit took place on 11 June.[22]

MacWhinney was nominated as the Republican candidate to contest the general election to be held on 29 October, 1924 for the constituency of Derry. The Unionist candidate, Malcolm M. MacNaughten of Port Ballintrae, Bushmills, was eager to find out something about his opponent. He wrote to Dawson Bates, Minister for Home Affairs:

> 'You will have seen that I am opposed by the egregious Galt (who of course does not matter at all – he can't get more than a handful of votes if as many) and an internee, MacWhinney who was an instructor in the Derry Technical School and is an adept at bomb making. If there is any information about MacWhinney which you could give me, it might be useful, for of course the people here know nothing about him except that he is an internee and that he is put up as a Republican.'

In reply Dawson Bates gave details of MacWhinney's involvement in the I.R.A. and of his time on the *Argenta*. He could not confirm if he was an expert in the making of bombs.[23]

Éamon de Valera, President of Sinn Féin was the Republican candidate for South Down. On 24 October he was arrested in Newry and sent back across the border. He travelled onto Sligo where he was scheduled to speak at a public meeting on Sunday the 26th. In Sligo he was joined on the platform by Madame Markievicz, Seán Lemass and Messrs J. Begley, E. O Donnell and S O Hanrahan. After leaving Sligo the party headed for Derry in two cars to attend a rally in support of MacWhinney in St. Columb's Hall. When they reached the border they abandoned the vehicles and proceeded on foot by a secondary road. However they were considerably behind schedule and the meeting which was timed for 8pm started without them. The two main speakers were Mr. J.L. Murrin and Mary MacSwiney who told the audience that it was her fifth speech that day. She urged those present to vote for MacWhinney, 'a Protestant born and bred in Ulster but now in Derry Jail.' As the time went by and there was still no sign of the de Valera party the speakers were forced to fill in the time as best they could. Mary MacSwiney made a second speech and another member of the platform party sang several patriotic songs. Shortly after 10pm word came through to the hall that de Valera had been arrested outside by a combined force of police and A Specials. He was brought to Belfast, lodged in Crumlin Road jail to await a court appearance.[24] On 1 November he was given a one month jail sentence.[25]

Sinn Féin described MacWhinney as 'one of those splendid types of northern Protestants who are republican by conviction and if elected he would be one of the greatest assets to the republican movement generally. His election ought to end definitely the religious and bigoted cry that Republicanism stands for any particular sect.'[26]

Seamus Black of 3 South Wall, Derry, MacWhinney's

election agent, was allowed to visit him in prison and the election address was approved by the Ministry of Home Affairs.[27] MacNaughten won the seat, securing 30,875 votes. MacWhinney received 5,869 with the Independent Galt in third place with just 517 votes. According to the *Belfast Telegraph* there was a good turnout of Republican supporters and some of the cars used by the MacWhinney activists were supplied from the Free State. Mr J.L. Murrin represented MacWhinney at the count. Unionists were returned for all thirteen Six County seats.[28]

In November 1924 MacWhinney and Hugh Corvin of 13, Hawthorne Street, Belfast, who also had been a candidate in the recent election were transferred from Derry to Belfast Prison. The Home Office had received information that 'an attempt might be made to release these and other Sinn Féin prisoners from Londonderry Prison, the attempt possibly being made to enter the prison by a ruse, and with the use of R.U.C. uniforms for this purpose.'[29]

MacWhinney spent only a few weeks in Belfast. He was released unconditionally on 15 December along with five others: Thomas Corrigan, Enniskillen; Hamilton Young, Belfast; James Byrne, Tullyorier, Co. Down and Frank Harper, Kilkeel. Hugh Corvin was released on 24 December.

Between March 1923 and November 1924, Mac Whinney corresponded by prison post cards with his friend, Hugh McCormick, a dentist, who resided at 25, Clarendon Street, Derry.[30] It is clear from this correspondence that MacWhinney was widely read, had many diverse interests and the police opinion of him as a man of superior intelligence is borne out by the evidence of these letters. Apparently he was allowed to write two cards a week. However, only the correspondence with Mc-Cormick has survived.

In the first postcard, dated 10 March 1923, he defends his refusal to accept conditional release:

'I much prefer to be a free man within walls than a convict on ticket of leave or bail outside, especially as I am by disposition as well as by religion a Protestant, and I am inspired by original sin to protest against what I regard as injustice and tyranny on the part of either the Pope, the British Empire or Belfast.' The following July, he wrote reaffirming his stance although he was aware that 'some of my friends in Dublin have been endeavouring to procure my release.'

Referring to the time prison life afforded him for reading he wrote:

'As I have unlimited time at my disposal and every prospect of these conditions continuing indefinitely so that no amount of reading matter seems capable of withstanding my assault, even monumental works like Gibbon's *Decline and Fall*, were it available, would only put me over a month or so ... ... You've asked me a couple of times if there is anything in the reading line I'm particularly interested in. Well I'm pretty nearly omnivorous, though if you've anything by Freud or any of his psychoanalytic disciples I'd be interested; also any of the recent books on radio telephony and as this start looks weird enough, I may as well continue the medley with Keats, Balzac, Swinbourne's second series of poems and ballads—I have his first here, and: Karl Marx! Of the latter it's said that his work is universally condemned by those who haven't read him. Still as I have said, I read anything from a Wild West shocker in an American magazine to *Dynamics of Rotating Bodies* by Williamson and Tarleton.'

Two writers MacWhinney disliked were Shakespeare and O.Henry. The lack of appreciation of Shakespeare he attributed to 'a too precocious acquaintance with unimportant details like variae lectiones of the Quarto and the folios and metrical peculiarities of the text which a misguided educational system thrust upon my unwilling mind.'

MacWhinney spent considerable time studying Irish in the prison and he has some interesting observations on Gaelic literature and the revival movement. It is obvious from the correspondence that he had some knowledge of the language before he was interned. He was very taken with the stories of Padraic Ó Conaire especially *Seacht mBua an Éirí Amach*. McCormick supplied him with Irish grammars and language aids. MacWhinney also wrote that 'Hegarty sent me in a couple of Irish books, the O Neill Lane is most useful and I have procured Fr Nolan's *Studies in Modern Irish*. He was very anxious to get any of Keating's works especially *Foras Feasa ar Éirinn*. He later commented: 'a grip of a language is a slow growth and I am anxious to acquire the capacity to express my ideas passably well in Gaelic. Not the least difficulty is the extraordinary limited vocabulary of modern writers: one has to go back to Keating if one wants to avoid long circumlocutions to express abstract ideas.' He was scathing in his comments on the lack of support at official level in the south of Ireland for Irish and he has interesting observations on the promotion of the various dialects:

> 'In view of all the fuss that is being made over Irish, it speaks badly for the sincerity or the intelligence of those who give the matter lip service, that we have not yet got a decent Irish-English nor English-Irish dictionary --- though a sum that an army contractor would regard as a moderate bribe would go far to getting one underway.--- As far as I can see all text books in Irish have their limitations: there is a tremendous amount of research work to be done and to be made available, and in spite of many protestations of zeal, nothing has yet been done officially towards repairing the destruction of the last 100 years.--- We are cursed with people yelling about the claims of this parish dialect and that parish dialect to be a standard of Gaelic pure and undefiled, while most of them fail to realise that it is a corrupt dialect they speak themselves – both in Irish and English. The last author who wrote in the Irish language and not in dialect is still almost unprocurable. Keating's Irish is as intelligible to Irish speakers as Shakespeare's English, of whom he was almost a contemporary, is to the English speaker. Imagine the folly of taking the modern dialect of Lancashire as a standard of English in preference to Shakespeare – and yet that is what these people are trying to insist on us doing.'

MacWhinney refers to a variety of topics throughout the correspondence. On freedom he commented: 'The desire for freedom must precede freedom' and: 'Fortunately a cage for the mind has not yet been devised.'

Writing on 15 April 1924 he referred to the Boundary Commission: 'I don't suppose for one moment that it will attain its object; both parties are too nervous about it--or should I say all three. If Lloyd George didn't 'settle' the Irish question he certainly simplified it by substituting a new and original source of trouble sufficiently virulent to obscure the original troubles: a sort of vaccine treatment giving rise to violent local inflammation.'

The following month he wrote in praise of the Irish poet AE: 'I notice AE is making a frenzied attack on the wild men of both sides lately. Now AE is a writer and thinker for whom I have the highest respect and is one of the most valuable if not the most valuable Irishman alive today, but if he thinks he can make any headway with a mad dog in trying to restore it to sanity by cogent reasoning and pure cold logic, I'm afraid he will be bitterly disappointed and will be lucky if he doesn't get infected with the rabies himself.'

On tourism he wrote: 'There are hundreds of places in Ireland that rival the tourist centres for scenery but most people only recognise beauty when they know where it is – hence the rush of the Philistines to places like Killarney and the Glens of Antrim.'

On the Roman Empire: 'It is a curious instance of the psychology of political prisoners, I suppose, that I find the history of Rome interesting in so far that I cannot get out of drawing parallels with a later empire on a similar model. I am almost convinced that the parallel will carry further. What a smash it will be and will we see it?—or survive it?'

On 25 December, 1923 he wrote that he 'wasn't greatly perturbed at spending another Christmas here, or even at the prospect of still another after this. In one sense it is a desperate waste of time, but on the other hand I have the advantages of unlimited leisure for thought, which I would never have in the ordinary way as I am inclined to mental laziness. I appear to be reaching a stage in which I can evolve some sort of order in a most untidy mental filing system. Christmas day is quite a treat here. It is chiefly distinguished by the fact that the gas is turned out an hour earlier in the evening– to provide time for reflection I suppose.'

Seven months before his release he commented: 'One gradually loses the time sense here, and you find yourself wondering whether an event happened a fortnight ago or three months.' He found the long dark days of winter irritating because the shortage of daylight curtailed his time for reading and study. On 21 April 1924, he wrote: ' Thank goodness, summertime begins again next week and by the end of this month the evenings will be fairly long; it is extraordinarily irritating to lose four or five hours a day all winter because the sun doesn't shine—a sort of caveman handicap.'

MacWhinney's last postcard to Hugh McCormick was written from Crumlin Road Jail, Belfast on Saturday 15 November 1924, a month before his release:

> 'I suppose you will be surprised to hear of my new abode, after being left so long in the cloistered seclusion of Derry. Sunday last I was informed of the change and I arrived here on the train Monday. Needless to say the reason for the change is a complete mystery. However I am beginning to settle down after the excitement of the journey—it is rather a novelty to see streets and people again after over two years, and how long more it is to last I don't know. I am sorry however to be so far removed from the kind offices of yourself and Pat in the way of literature but one can't have everything. I left a parcel of five books in charge of the chief warder to be called for, with a list on the wrapper.'

Soon after his release MacWhinney came to Dublin where he was appointed to the executive of the Sinn Féin party.[31] For a time he was the Chief Inspector of Patents and later a Factory Inspector.

Linda and Wilson were married in St. Michan's Catholic Church Halston Street, Dublin by Rev Laurence F. Kelly. The Pro-Cathedral was Linda's choice but she was not allowed to have her wedding there because Wilson was not a Catholic. When she threatened to get married in the Registry Office in Ormond Quay a compromise was reached-- the ceremony could take place in another parish. In the event Linda and Wilson were married in the sacristy of the church. Francis McLoughlin Scannell was the best man and the bride's maid was Annie McGloin, Linda's niece. Annie was daughter of Robert and Julia McGloin of Kinlough, Co. Leitrim. Neither flowers nor photographs were permitted. Among the presents they received was a beautiful silver tray presented by the North Dublin Fianna Fáil organisation.

The couple resided in Linda's home, No.29, which also operated as a Nurses' Co-op. The following year, in November, their only child, Ann was born. Mary, Linda's sister and Dr. McCarthy were the sponsors at the baptism. However Mary was unable to attend and Dorothy Macardle 'did proxy' for her. Dorothy took a great interest in Ann's welfare and she was especially supportive of her during Linda's final illness and at the time of her death. Dr McCarthy was Deputy Resident Medical Superintendent of Grangegorman Mental Hospital. He later took up employment in St Columba's Mental Hospital in Sligo.[32]

The first years of the marriage were content. Wilson had his own workshop in the house where he put his marvellous and varied talents to use. Here he made radio sets and items of furniture including a beautiful desk to which he fitted a number of light bars. Linda was busy running the co-op, taking the phonecalls for the nurses. She also continued her round of meetings, political and voluntary. The couple often went on picnics to the Wicklow mountains in Wilson's Bently and for a time they bred Alsations.

After about ten years of marriage, Linda and Wilson began to drift apart. In the opinion of their daughter, Ann, Wilson had grown tired of people continually calling to their home 'looking for Linda Kearns.' Early in 1941, when Ann herself became very seriously ill with a brain tumour, which necessitated a lengthy stay in the Richmond Hospital, Linda and Wilson visited her separately.[33] Linda spent endless hours at her daughter's bedside and she said later that this ordeal brought back memories of some of her worst moments as a prisoner. Indeed after a visit to the hospital she was so upset and disoriented that she went astray on her way back home to Gardiner Place.[34] Ann was in the Richmond when German bombs fell on the North Strand in Dublin. This was a further worry for Linda and she decided that when Ann recovered, she would send her to secondary school outside of the city. Apparently Wilson was totally opposed to this idea and relations between him and Linda worsened. Linda had her way however and Ann was sent as a boarder to the Ursuline Convent in Sligo.[35] She was there from 1942 to 1947.

However the event that finally broke the marriage involved one of the women staying in Linda's house. She was Bets Conroy, a relation of the famous writer Padraic Ó Conaire. Wilson began an affair with her and Linda told them to leave.[36] Wilson and Bets went to live in Ranelagh where they resided up to the time of his death some thirty years later. Wilson's working life as a factory inspector continued until he was seventy. He was permitted this extension by virtue of the fact that he was a veteran of the War of Independence. A great cycling enthusiast, he regularly cycled across the city from his home to his newsagents, Kirwans on the corner of Parnell Street and Belvedere Row. He owned three machines: a *Jack Taylor* for long distances, a *Paris* for wet weather and a *Claude Butler* for fine conditions.

Around 1968 he contracted glaucoma and his sight began to fail. He died on 23 August, 1970. Bets survived him by a number of years.[37]

Chapter Nine
Nursing Issues

Linda Kearns' involvement at a high level with the most powerful political party in the country undoubtedly ensured that other avenues of interest and influence opened up to her. Two years after Fianna Fáil came to power she was appointed to the General Nursing Council, a statutory body and forerunner of An Bord Altranais. In 1936 the Minister for Justice appointed her to the visiting committee of Mountjoy Prison and in 1939 she was a government appointee to the newly formed Irish Red Cross. In all probability her weekly column on the Woman's Page of *The Irish Press* came about as a result of her political connections. It is important to remember that old friendships dating back to the War of Independence continued especially with de Valera and Gerry Boland. There is no doubt also that she used her political and nursing influence to the advantage of members of her own family. This manifested itself in the securing of jobs and also in assisting relations engaged in the cattle trade especially during the Economic War in the 1930s.[1]

However it would be utterly wrong to assume that Linda's achievements derived solely and entirely from her political associations. The record of her work particularly in the area of nursing show her as person of great ability, strong conviction and dedication in the pursuit of her objectives. Throughout the 30s and 40s she was recognised as an influential nurses' leader. Apart from sitting on the General Nursing Council she was secretary of the Irish Nurses Association, and also a member of the National Council of Nurses. In 1933 she headed a delegation of some eighty nurses from the Free State at the International Council of Nurses in Paris and Brussels. At that time she was honorary treasurer of the National Council of Trained Nurses of the Free State and secretary of the Irish Nurses' Association. On Tuesday, 10 July, in Paris, she read a paper entitled: 'When should the probationer be allowed to take part in the routine work of the hospital ward?' The following Friday, after the delegates were welcomed by M. Hymans, Belgian Minister of Foreign Affairs, she presided over the meeting of the Congress in Brussels. At the conclusion of the Congress most of the nurses from Ireland took part in a pilgrimage to Lourdes.[2]

The Irish Nurses' Association grew out of the Dublin Nurses' Club which was founded in 1900. A few years later it was felt desirable to extend the Club in order to extend membership to nurses outside the capital. The headquarters of the Association was at 86 Lower Leeson Street. In its early years its activities were three-fold; lectures on medical questions; outdoor and indoor entertainment for its members and the pursuit of nurses' objectives such as state registration. During the time in which Linda was secretary and Molly Feenan president, the association, which had lost some of its earlier vigour, was revitalised. Representations were regularly made to the minister for Local Government on various issues such as salaries, working hours and conditions in certain medical institutions. The policy of providing lectures was continued. In the 1940s Linda worked through the Irish Nurses' Association in her efforts to establish a holiday home for nurses.[3]

Linda was a government appointee on the General Nursing Council for the term beginning on 1 February 1934. Among some of the best known members of the Council at that time were; Sir Edward Cooey Bigger M.D. chairman; Dr. J.M. O'Donovan, Dr. W. Fallon Dr. P. MacCarville and Miss Halbert, R.G.N.[4] This Council was set up under the *Nurses Registration (Ireland) Act, 1919*. It met for the first time in February, 1920. Initially, membership was by appointment only and then in 1924 Government appointees were joined by elected members.[5] The main responsibilities of the Council were to keep a registry of nurses and to formulate the rules regarding training hospitals and nursing examinations. It also discussed standards in various hospitals and could recommend the closure of wards if that was deemed necessary. For example at the meeting of 16 November 1938 the Council criticized the method of sterilising surgical instruments in the South Cork Co. Hospital pointing out that 'the present system... by use of a pan on a kitchen fire must be abolished and instead each ward should have at least a fish kettle and a gas ring for that purpose.'[6]

The General Nursing Council met twice a year at 75 Merrion Square, Dublin but occasionally a special meeting might be called if some urgent matter necessitated a discussion. One such meeting, which was convened at Linda's request in January 1938, applied to the Returning Officer for the Seanad elections to have the General Nursing Council admitted to the register of nominating bodies. Linda explained that as the new Seanad was to be vocational in structure, the Council representing so large a number of nurses would have a special claim. The members decided to make application under the Cultural and Educational panel and Linda and the chairman Dr. Cooey Biggar were chosen to go forward for election.[7] The returning officer turned down the application on the grounds that 'the professional interests of which the General Nursing Council is representative were not among those defined by law to be the professional interests for the purposes of the Cultural and Educational panel.' An appeal was lodged with the Clerk of the Dáil but was rejected by the Appeal Committee.[8]

Among other issues on which Linda expressed views were the representation on the Council for private nurses and whether sanatoria should be given training status. At the meeting of 7April 1943, she said that private nurses should not be represented by matrons or assistant matrons. She proposed that they be represented by 'two registered nurses (not being nor having been matrons, assistant matrons or tutor sisters of hospitals) who are, or have been engaged in private practice.'[9] A special meeting, at which Linda was not present, was called to discuss this change in the regulations. Her motion was declared null and void on the grounds that it had not been formally put on the agenda.[10] One of the private nurses' representatives on the Council was Annie P Smithson who supported the decision not to sanction sanatoria as training schools.[11]

Linda was a strong advocate of ongoing training for nurses but she thought it advisable that a limit be put on the number of girls allowed to do nursing. Her concern was that many of them could find themselves unemployed.

The provision of a pension fund for nurses was an objective which Linda and other nurses' leaders worked hard to achieve throughout the 30s and 40s. It was an issue which, although supported by many leading members of the medical profession, was dogged by refusal and evasion on the part of government. The campaign really began in 1929 when Miss Healy of the Irish Nurses' Union called for a National Pension Fund for nurses, emphasising that it could be achieved if a united front was presented.[12] An attempt was made to start a pension fund among the nurses themselves by asking each member on the General Nursing Register to subscribe a small sum. However the response was small; the scheme had to be abandoned and the contributions were returned to the subscribers.[13]

Nurses saw the *Hospital Bill 1933* as another opportunity to press their claim for a pension scheme. Each T.D. and senator was asked to support an amendment to the Bill that a sum of money be allocated from the Hospital Sweepstakes for this purpose. The amendment was withdrawn at the request of the parliamentary secretary in the Department of Health, who promised that he would investigate the matter again after consultation with representatives of the nursing bodies. Two years later the Senate passed a private bill–*The Nurses' and Midwives' Pensions' Bill, 1935* which had been drafted free of charge by Mr. S. Brown K.C. and put forward by Sir Edward

Cooey Biggar. However by the time the bill went to the Dáil it was declared to be dead because the Senate was abolished in the meantime.[14] The response of Seán T O'Kelly, Minister for Local Government and Public Health to the Senate initiative was not encouraging: 'the Government did not propose adopting as a Government measure the *Nurses' and Midwives' Pensions Bill*.'[15]

Despite this set-back the campaign went on. Questionnaires were sent to every nurse on the register. However the result was discouraging. There were only 2,440 replies out of a total of 7,400 questionnaires sent out between May and October 1937. Then in late 1938 it was decided that 'the three women senators and the three deputies should meet together in the Ladies' room of Leinster House to discuss the pension scheme.' As a result of this initiative, Senators Helena Concannon and Margaret Pearse set up a meeting between Nurses' leaders and Dr. Ward, parliamentary secretary. Ward said that a pension scheme would have to be investigated by an actuary and then the government might give it consideration.

On 1 March, 1939 Linda addressed a largely attended meeting, chaired by Miss Healy, President of the I.N.O. in Jury's Hotel, Dublin. Linda's proposal– that influential people including members of the medical profession be requested to approach the Minister for Health on the matter of a pension scheme– was adopted by the meeting. Following on this decision a circular outlining the history of the struggle for a pension and the justness of the nurses' demand, was sent to every T.D. in the Dáil by the Irish Nurses' Organisation.[16]

> For the past ten years our organisation has been agitating for a Pension Scheme for nurses. How necessary such a scheme is, may be judged by the number of elderly or invalid nurses who are not able to work and are practically destitute after many years of service for others. Nurses do not come under the unemployment scheme, and the National Health will only apply to them for a certain period after which they may

have the Disability of 7/6 per week upon which to exist until they reach the age of seventy and are eligible for the Old Age Pension.

We would ask if the nation does not consider that Irish nurses are worthy of a better pension than that of 10/- a week. How many lives have these women saved during their years of service? How many hours have they spent fighting for those lives by day and night? The work too in Public Health is of inestimable value for the State; while the midwife has the care of two lives as she goes forth in all hours and in all weathers when the call comes. What could ever pay these nurses for their work?[17]

During the summer of 1939 Kathleen Nix of the I.N.O. travelled all over the country meeting nurses' groups in an attempt to muster support for the pension scheme and an increase in salaries.[18] The rate of pay at that time varied from one county to another. For example in the Tipperary, South Riding health district a nurse started with a salary of £70 per annum rising by annual increments of £3 to £85 a year. A nurse with Central Midwives' Board qualifications started at £80 rising to a maximum of £95 per annum.[19]

Over the next few years meetings were organised such as that on 29 May 1943, addressed by Alderman Doyle T.D., Lord Mayor of Dublin, Dr. J. P. Brennan, Coroner for South Dublin, Surgeon Barniville, Dr. Patrick MacCarville and Dr. Kerry Reddin. Seán Ó hUadhaigh the honorary solicitor to the I.N.O. said it was a disgrace that anyone should have to work on continuous night duty for 20 years as some nurses had to do. Such a state of affairs could only be rectified when nurses were properly organised.[20] The following October Seán MacEntee, Minister for Health received a deputation consisting of officers of the main nursing organisations. The Irish Nurses' Association was represented by Mollie Feenan, president and Linda, secretary; Nellie Healy, Eleanor Grogan and Kathleen Nix

Annual Concert

AT MOUNTJOY PRISON

Sunday, 4th January, 1942

Programme

1. Mr. Jimmy Campbell and Theatre Royal Orchestra with Miss Peggy Dell, John Lynsky, Harry Bailey, John Torney, Noel Purcell and Roy Irving
2. Recital by No. 1 Army Band.
   Conductor: Lieutenant J. G. Doherty.

PART I.

Selection: Gems of Irish Song	arr. W. Wright
Cornet Solo: "The Lost Chord"	Sullivan
Medley: Community Medley.	arr. Debroy Somers

3. Mr. Robert McCullagh ... Song
4. Mr. Val Vousden ... Entertainer
5. Mr. Joe Carey ... Accordeonist
6. Miss Joan Reddin ... Song
7. Jesson and Farrelly ... Dancers
8. Jim Jonson and Vernon Hayden ... Comedians
9. Mr. Michael O'Higgins ... Song
10. Mr. Jimmy O'Dea in a Comedy Sketch
11. Miss May Devitt ... Song
12. Mr. Norman Barr ... Magician
13. Mr. Christopher Casson ... Songs with the Harp
14. Mr. Al. Thomas ... Recitation
15. Mr. Hilton Edwards and Members of the Gate Theatre Company present "Clementine"
16. Mr. Larry Daniel ... Song
17. Mr. Jack Maguire ... Violinist
18. Micheál MacLiammóir
19. Mr. Tyrell Pine ... One Man Concert Party
20. Army Band Recital: Part II.
    March Selection: "Passing of the Regiments" ... arr. Winter

NATIONAL ANTHEM

Compère: MR. J. ERIC HENRY

Sample of programme for the Annual Christmas Concert at Mountjoy

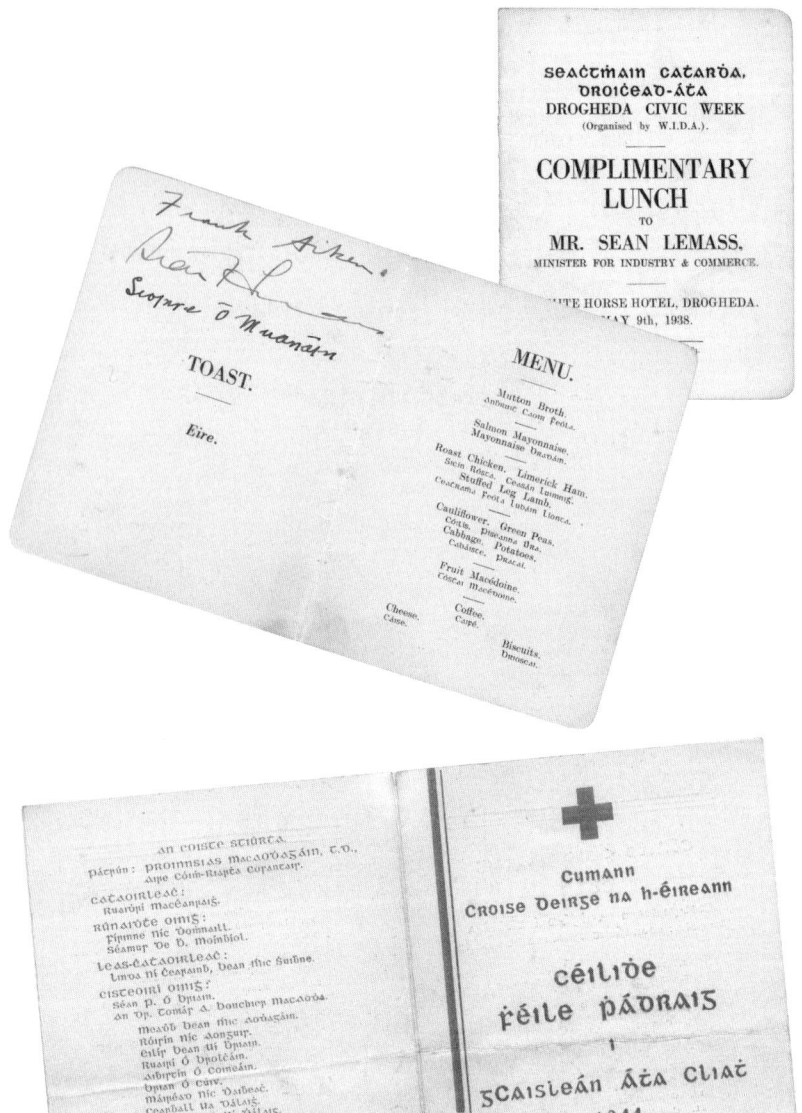

Memorabilia kept by Linda

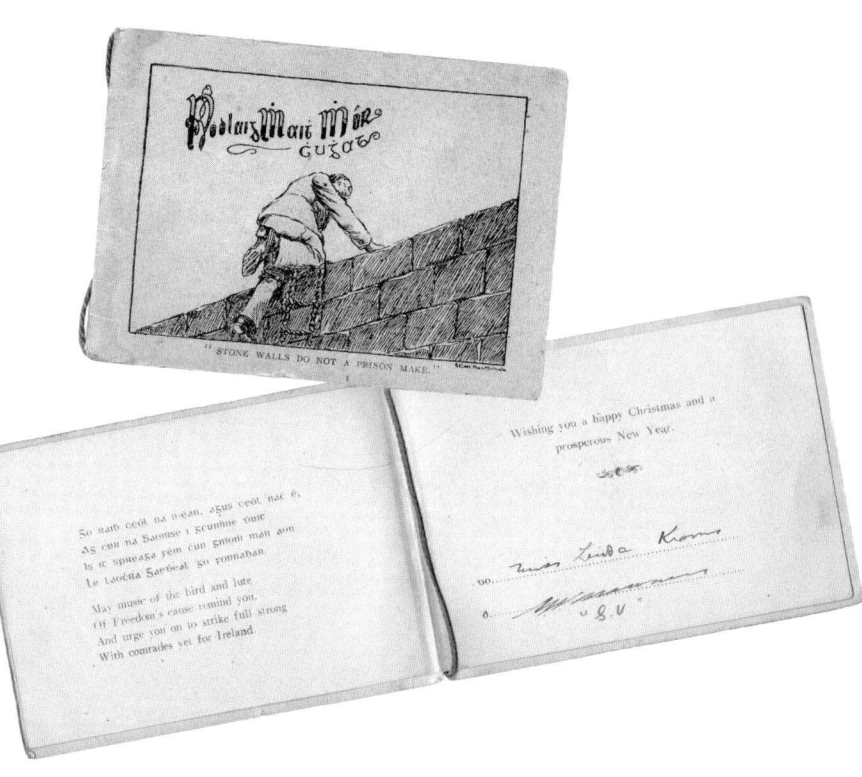

Memorabilia kept by Linda

Early photo of Linda

Linda's husband,
Wilson MacWhinney as a youth

Linda with her daughter Ann

Linda with her daughter Ann

Picnic photo of Linda

Dorothy Macardle, 1952

Linda with her daughter Ann in Glengarriff

Linda with Yvonne Heutsch of the Red Cross, Geneva

Linda in a photo taken by her husband.
The bookcase with lighted glass bars was made by Wilson

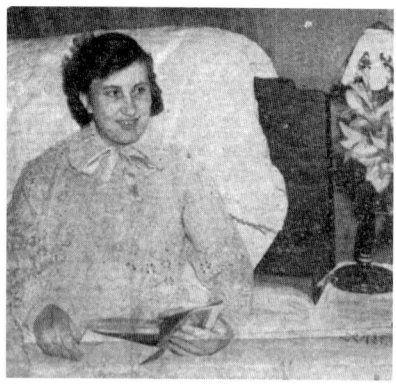

Linda's cousin Mary Kearns, modelling for *Penelope* column

Committee Kilrock Holiday Home, Howth, 1946
Top Row - Miss Young, Mr.Hogan (sec.), Mr.Davy, Miss O'Rourke, Miss Considine, Mr.McGarry, Miss O'Flaherty
Bottom Row - Miss Feenan, Dr.Reddin, Mrs. K.Nix, Dr. C.Ward, Mrs. McWhinney, Dr. McCartan, Miss Cullen and Miss Delaney in centre

Linda's Grave, Glasnevin Cemetary

represented the I.N.O.; The Matrons' Association and the Irish Guild of Catholic Nurses were represented respectively by Miss Stokes of Baggot St. Hospital and Miss Young, Joint Honorary Secretary. McEntee told the deputation that there had been a very poor response to the questionnaire which had been sent to nurses during the tenure of office of his predecessor Seán T.O'Kelly. Miss Grogan countered by saying that at that time the membership of the I.N.O. had been very small but this situation had greatly improved in the intervening years. According to McEntee the government was a sympathetic to the introduction of a pension scheme but he feared that the cost could be prohibitive. 'However, he would see what could be done when a joint nurses' committee had got together and presented in coordinated form, the necessary data for the formulation of such a scheme, after which he would be prepared to discuss the matter again.' In regard to other points raised at the meeting he said that he was in favour of a 96-hour fortnight and the abolition of continuous night duty. The question of whether a nurse falling ill should or should not be treated free in a hospital controlled by the employing authority was altogether a matter for that authority. Nurses' salaries, being State aided, bore a relation to the rate collected in the counties in which they were employed and so it followed that there was a discrepancy in the scale of salaries paid in different counties.[21]

The government failure to deliver on a pension for all nurses provoked a stinging editorial in *The Irish Nurses' Magazine* in June 1945. The writer referred to an article in the *Irish Times* sometime previously which highlighted the disgracefully low remuneration of primary teachers asserting that it brought shame upon Ireland.

> 'Well we should like to substitute our own profession for that of the teachers (or with more propriety and justice add the one to the other) and borrowing the expostulations of the *Irish Times* about the unfair and callous and obscurantist treatment of teachers, ascribe them to the exactly similar

treatment of a not less deserving, long-suffering and hard-working body – namely the nurses of Ireland. Speaking of the salary of teachers (who badly off as they are, are better off than nurses), the *Irish Times* says that "the payment of such stipends" (we like the word 'stipend' –it is so apropos!), "is not merely a national disgrace – it paves the way for a national disaster." Pari passu that also goes, without the change of a syllable, for the nursing profession.'

The writer went on to accuse the government of a parsimonious spirit as far as nurses were concerned. 'Thrift, economy, a prudent surveillance of expenditure, a wise adjustment of means to ends there always must be, ... but a parsimonious attitude to life never got a man, a party, a government or a nation anywhere.'

Linda Kearns' own views on nurses and the nursing profession can be gleaned from a lecture entitled *'The Life of a Nurse'* which she gave to a meeting of the Irish Women Citizens' Association chaired by Mrs. Jean Coote at No.5, Leinster Street, Dublin. On the pensions' question, she said that the Hospitals' Commission should devise a scheme on a contributory basis so that nurses could retire at the age of fifty. She had a grievance against the hospitals for turning out too many nurses in the year. These hospitals 'take the girls in, get free labour from them and never ask what happens their nurses when they leave. After training, about 30% find work, 20% marry in their first year of employment and the remaining 50% become private nurses. These private nurses in particular suffered most from the system. On average they secured work for only seven months of the year and this was usually night duty, involving the nursing of chronic cases with no hope of recovery. The number of nurses allowed to return from England to take up employment in Ireland should be reduced. The average nurse does not marry, for the simple reason that she does not get the opportunity of meeting people. I have known nurses who spent much money on new dresses for a dance and who, at the last moment had to go on duty. There are at the moment a number of nurses on the verge of starvation, especially the older nurses. They deserve much more from their country than that.' In answer to a question from a member of the audience she said that in her opinion the average patient preferred a lay nurse to a nun and the proposal to give complete control to nuns in the Dublin Union was a very serious matter for the nurses employed there.[22]

Privately, Linda disagreed with nuns working in hospitals, feeling that they should conduct their lives within their convents. This attitude stemmed largely from the fact that lay nurses found it difficult if not impossible to achieve senior positions in hospitals controlled by nuns. She probably also shared a view that was prevalent among lay nurses who cared for old people in institutions such as the South Dublin Union namely that some nuns were reluctant, in the interests of economy, to change the sheets of very ill or dying patients. Instead they preferred to say the rosary rather than make the patient comfortable.[23]

Linda was a government appointee to the Irish Red Cross Society which was established in September 1939 under the presidency of Dr. Douglas Hyde, President of Ireland. The objectives of the Red Cross were:

1. To furnish voluntary aid to the sick and wounded of armies in time of war.
2. To furnish relief to prisoners of war.
3. In time of peace or war to carry on and assist in work for the improvement of health, the prevention of disease and the mitigation of suffering throughout the world.

The need for such a society as the Red Cross in Ireland was highlighted by the fact that only a few days before its establishment over four hundred victims of war landed in the country.

Linda was a member of the first Central Council of the Society which was nominated by the government and among the other officers were: Dr. Charles J. Mac

Auley,(chairman), The Hon. W.E. Wylie K.C.(vice-chairman), Áine Bean E Ceannt and Senator D.L. Robinson (treasurers), Annie M.P. Smithson, Helena Moloney, Mary E.Hackett, Dr. T.J. O'Connell Secretary, I.N.T.O., Colonel T.J. McKinney, Director of Medical Services., Viscountess Powerscourt and Dr. Patrick Mac Carville.

Frank Aiken, Minister for Coordination of Military and Civil Defence told the first meeting that Dr. Hyde had informed the Taoiseach, Éamon De Valera that he would be donating £500 to the Society and that the government had given £1000 to assist the Council in purchasing a premises.

'Unfortunately Europe is engaged in an awful holocaust and although we are not engaged in it, the Irish Red Cross Society will have very valuable work to do, first in organising the voluntary aid for the sick and the wounded– a body which can give aid in that way to our own army if it ever became engaged– and secondly, in the present circumstances of Europe it may have very valuable work to do in looking after sick or wounded or refugees who may unfortunately reach our shores.'

Aiken referred to the sinking of the *Athenia* on the very first day of the War, an event which highlighted the necessity for the Red Cross in Ireland.[24]

Linda was vice-chairperson of the committee that administered the Emergency Hospital Supplies Depot at 7 Cavendish Row, Dublin. The other members were; The Duchess of St. Albans, (chairperson), Colonel Thomas J McKinney,(secretary), Lady Talbot de Malahide (treasurer), Miss Hackett and Miss Overend. Initially the function of the depot was to produce knitted articles such as pullovers, jumpers and socks for shipwrecked sailors. It also had the responsibility for the purchase of shirting, wool, pyjamas and bandage material. These materials were then sent to sub-depots throughout the country and the finished products were returned to Dublin from where distribution was organised.[25]

The layout of 7 Cavendish Row, a Georgian house was described by one of the volunteer workers:

' ... the workrooms are in the grand reception rooms upstairs; on upper floors are store rooms and a cosy little kitchen where workers can revive themselves with tea. On the ground floor are the office and a receiving and sorting room for parcels. Down in the depths of the basement is what remains of a ton of plaster of Paris. Ultra cleanliness and strict economy are two points impressed on every newcomer. When I had put on my cap and overall and scrubbed my hands and forearms with strong pink soap they set me at folding pieces of blay to make cases for dressings. You fold one end, smooth it flat and detach any frayed threads that might catch in the sewing machine. Thinking to myself that efficiency tells even in the simplest tasks, I worked full steam ahead, casting any loose threads heedlessly on the floor. When the room superintendent came round she was pained. None of that frayed out thread would now be hygienic enough to use as stuffing for pillows! And so I learned the first lesson of nothing wasted. A sympathetic worker said that she did worse on her first day—she put her handbag down on the sterilised table. In the basements are bags and bags of plaster of Paris. A little at a time is baked in a biscuit tin till it is free of lumps; then each worker takes her own supply on a tray and wearing rubber gloves she rubs and rubs the powder into the long gauze bandages. A four inch bandage when rolled must weigh not less than five and not more than six ounces, and any that do not pass are rolled again. The finished bandages are packed in tins and it is one worker's job to seal the tins with wax and write the date on each, because the plaster should not be kept too long. The shell dressings comprised pads of lint or cotton in various sizes stitched to bandages which were ingeniously pleated so that they could be opened quickly without touching the part that goes on the wound. These were mostly made in the sub-depots and then sent back to Dublin to be sterilized and packed in cellophane. The finished products were stamped

Irish Red Cross and recorded in the 'Consignments Out' book.[26]

On 6 October, 1940 Linda visited Manorhamilton, Co. Leitrim to review North Leitrim units of the Local Security Force (L.S.F) and the Red Cross. 1,500 men and 400 women and girls filed past. Some of the men she had known in the War of Independence. She also recognised a doctor who was 'no laggard when his skill was needed twenty years ago.'[27]

The Red Cross in Dublin was faced with a very serious situation when the North Strand was bombed by the German Airforce on 31 May 1941 leaving thirty four dead and ninety injured. Three hundred houses were destroyed or damaged. At the first meeting of the central council of the organisation after the bombing it was reported that the Dublin Red Cross had provided care and shelter for almost nine hundred people in five locations; Baggotsrath Hall, Y.M.C.A., St. George's Hall, Mespil Road and the Mansion House. Forty five thousand meals had been prepared and served. Approximately one thousand two hundred individuals had received ten thousand items of clothing. A few weeks earlier in two separate air raids, Belfast had suffered the loss of nine hundred people with over four hundred injured. Red Cross assistance from Dublin had amounted to over £6000. It is unlikely that Linda was heavily involved in the Red Cross work because during these weeks her daughter Ann was dangerously ill in hospital. Incidentally the Germans admitted responsibility and £327,000 was paid over to the Irish Government in 1958.

Linda was also a member of the Deportees' Committee which met in 41 Parnell Square, Dublin to give assistance to those deported from England as a result of the I.R.A. bombing campaign. However the following letter quoted in Tim Pat Coogan's *The I.R.A.* demonstrates the ineffectiveness of the Committee due to lack of funds.[28]

14/8/1940.

A Chara,

We enclose P.O. for ten shillings. We regret to state that this fund is now completely exhausted and except money is forthcoming from an unexpected source, you cannot expect any remittance next week, or will you, we're afraid, any further remittance from this committee. We extremely regret the necessity for sending this notice to you, but we have exhausted every source known to us. If, in the future, we see any prospect of getting further help for you, we shall communicate with you.

Yours sincerely ,

L. Kearns MacWhinney	Agnes McCullough
Una de Staic	Helena Molony

In August 1950, Linda's name was put forward by the Irish Red Cross as a candidate for the Florence Nightingale medal to the International Committee in Geneva. Details of her nursing training and career as a nurse both as a practitioner and as a representative were submitted. Her work with the Red Cross involved the organisation 'of some of the counties throughout Ireland with the General Secretary. Gave courses of lectures and examined members of the Irish Red Cross for their First Aid and Home Nursing Certificates. Served on various Red Cross committees.' She was awarded the medal on 12 May, 1951 just over three weeks before she died. The presentation was made to her on her deathbed.

Chapter Ten
Visiting Committee

Linda was a visiting justice of Mountjoy Jail, Dublin for fifteen years. After her appointment by the Department of Justice she attended her first meeting on 3 February, 1936 and continued as a member until her final illness in 1951. The visiting committee consisted of ten members, four of whom were women. The other three women in the first years of Linda's term were: Miss E. Condell, 6 Frankfort Avenue, Rathgar, Miss Angela Boland, 36A Merrion Square and Mrs M.E. Lindsay, 88 Lower Leeson Street.

Meetings were held monthly and were attended by the governor who in 1936 was Seán Kavanagh, and who, like Linda, had been a prisoner in Mountjoy during the War of Independence. An official inspection of the jail took place in conjunction with the meeting. Wards, workshops, cookhouses, laundry, woodyards, exercise yards, bakery and hospital were visited. Prisoners were entitled to present their complaints in person. Members of the committee made special efforts to make contact with prisoners who were under sentence of death and those on hunger strike. Apart from the monthly inspection individual members made unannounced visits and then wrote their report in the Visiting Committee Book. Many of these visits were made to coincide with the time of the preparation of meals so that a report could be issued on the quality of food being served to the prisoners.[1] Linda made her first private visit a month after her appointment and although her report was favourable she later was quite critical of several aspects of prison life.[2] Many of her recommendations including one to augment the stock of books in the library, were not put into effect until years later.

Linda was particularly concerned with the standard of care for sick prisoners and also with the type of accommodation provided for the female warders. Her most important criticisms were deemed significant enough to be appended to the annual report for 1938.[3] She complained that B wing of the prison which housed the hospital patients was completely unsuitable in that it faced northwards and consequently got little sunlight. It was dangerous in her opinion to have sick prisoners and healthy prisoners in close proximity in the same wing. The cells in B wing were badly ventilated, badly lit and not suitable for patients especially those suffering from tuberculosis or venereal disease. No hot water was available in this wing and patients had to walk through a long draughty passage to have a bath. She maintained that when she herself had been a prisoner in Mountjoy, 'there were facilities which the patients are now deprived of. At that time there was a constant supply of hot water and wards suitable for the sick with proper windows and ventilation.' She emphasized that no progress had been made in the intervening nineteen years. Her recommendation was that a small hospital be built with proper medical equipment for the resident medical officer. On a previous occasion, Linda had criticised the practice of carrying the sick prisoners' meals, uncovered, across open ground where they were exposed to all kinds of weather and were usually cold by the time they reached their destination.[4]

In her report Linda also found fault with the newly acquired electric cooker which was not even as large as 'a small family cooker' and which was used only twice a week and never after 5pm. In regard to the living quarters of the female warders she described them as dull, dreary, lacking sunlight. 'When women are continuously employed in the arduous work of minding prisoners it is essential that their home should be bright and cheerful and everything should be done to create an atmosphere of peace and comfort.' She felt that new accommodation for the female staff could be built at the same time as a hospital.

Linda's report drew a negative response from the Department of Justice. Mr. Hurley, its superintending officer attended the next meeting of the committee and told the members that the medical adviser to the department was satisfied that the Mountjoy facilities were adequate 'for dealing with ordinary cases of illness' and that official sanction for a new hospital even if it was required would not be forthcoming due to financial constraints. Linda disagreed with the view of the department although the chairman of the committee P.S. Doyle T.D. declared himself satisfied with Mr. Hurley's response. The Mountjoy M.O. Dr. O'Sullivan attended the meeting but apparently made no comment.[5]

In July 1936, Linda attended the inaugural meeting of the Commission of Inquiry into the Treatment of Political Prisoners. Madame McBride is reported as saying that that she trusted that the Commission would be instrumental in establishing a standard of political treatment which both the government and the prisoners could recognise. Mrs Elgin O'Rahilly was appointed Honorary Secretary to the Commission. Mrs Hanna Sheehy Skeffington also attended the meeting. As far as the Mountjoy Visiting Committee was concerned the question of political prisoners in the prison was a difficult one not because there was a history of ill treatment but rather on account of the tension between them and ordinary prisoners. The latter were resentful of the fact that the political prisoners received extra privileges and the members of the visiting committee were unanimously of the opinion that the only solution was to transfer the I.R.A. men from Mountjoy to another prison.[6]

A serious riot took place on 2 March 1940 which resulted in injuries and which necessitated calling in the Gardaí.[7] The eight political prisoners tore off their bedsteads and used them as a barricade across the ward. Tables and chairs were used as missiles. One of those involved was Tomás MacCurtain, son of the Lord Mayor of Cork who had been murdered by members of the British forces in the War of Independence. MacCurtain was under sentence of death for the murder of Detective Officer Roche in Cork.[8] Although he was on hunger strike at the time he told a member of the visiting committee who spoke to him the day after the disturbances that he felt better than he did before the 'scrap'! He had sustained slight injuries but he was anxious to assure his relatives that he did not require the services of an outside doctor. No punishment was meted out in the aftermath of the riot, a decision which was deemed very wise by the visiting committee. Linda visited MacCurtain and Thomas Grogan who was also on hunger strike a couple of weeks after the riot:

'At the request of friends and relatives of the two prisoners on hunger strike I visited them today to enquire the exact reason of their hunger strike. Tomás MacCurtain told me the original purpose of the hunger strike was to ensure that all men sentenced by the Special Criminal Court, including those sentenced to penal servitude, would automatically be transferred to military custody. He also informed me that he personally would be satisfied to serve a term of penal servitude in a civil prison provided he was given full political treatment. Thomas Grogan insists on transfer to a military prison and will remain on hunger strike until this is granted to those sentenced to penal servitude.'[9]

MacCurtain was removed to St. Bricin's hospital. On 19 April he gave up his hunger strike but was still under sentence of death. Strenuous efforts were made to avert his execution especially by his counsel and by Seán T. Ó Ceallaigh. On 10 July his sentence of death was commuted to penal servitude for life by de Valera for reasons that are still not known.[10] One theory of many is that Sinéad de Valera exerted considerable pressure on her husband, not to go through with the execution.

The visiting committee succeeded in bringing about significant changes in the prison routine in the years 1945-47. One new member, Christopher E. Reddin of 85, Morehampton Road, Dublin, with whom Linda worked closely on a sub-committee, was particularly effective in this regard. The reason for his success was largely due to his meticulous research which he presented in writing for comment by the committee. His observations of prisoners and prison life make interesting reading:

> 'It is of interest to note in view of the recent criticisms of Éire prisons, that prisoners coming from middle class homes or with professional backgrounds like Jerome O'Sullivan, Orwell Road, Rathgar, Sydney Cooper, the solicitor, ex detective J. Sherlock have no complaint against the application of the prison rules and regulations.'

According to Reddin the reasons for this were that these prisoners were usually educated and therefore they made full use of library facilities. Furthermore their social background 'makes them avoid association with undesireable prison inmates.' Reddin made it a point to interview prisoners and members of the staff including the governor and to document their views and responses. He came to the conclusion that radical changes should take place as regards prisoners' exercise, education and recreation. He wrote: 'Exercise consists mainly of moping around exercise compounds or standing or sitting in huddled groups in shelters.' He maintained that many prisoners slept badly because there was a lack of proper physical exercise. On one of his first visits to the prison he had seen prisoners using a ball made of wrapped around rags for their game of football. Reddin had an extended conversation with one the staff who told him that a juvenile who after serving his two month sentence declared on leaving that he knew all about 'the water method' of abortion. Another who had served his sentence for sexual perversion was believed to have 'signed up' five young prisoners 'to accommodate him in his proposed continued life of sex perversion after he and they left the prison.' Reddin was told that 'self abuse' was the great tragedy of juvenile prison life and that prisoners' conversation was dominated by the subject of sex. There were really only two other topics of conversation: 'the jobs they had done and the jobs they intended to do when they got out.' Crime, he was told, was the only occupation for which you didn't need a reference.[11]

In December 1946, Reddin, Linda and another committee member Mr. J.J. Sheil, a solicitor, sat as a sub-committee which met a number of times, to investigate the possibility of providing lectures, films and better library facilities for the prisoners.[12] The number of books available to prisoners was found to be 900 whereas it had been 4000 before the war. It was discovered also that A class inmates liked books of an 'escapist' character! The sub-committee decided to seek a capital advance from the Department of Justice and to secure books from the Dublin City Library and from the Hospital Library Council. The chief executive officer of Dublin Education Committee was to be approached regarding the organising of lectures and craft classes.

Major changes were put in place in 1947. The first film was shown on 3 June and was deemed a 'complete success.' The Department of Justice advanced £500 for the purchase of library books and gave a further grant of £300 the following year. The prisoners were allowed food parcels three times a year; at Christmas, Easter and Hallow E'en. Radio sets and extension speakers were provided and the sum of money payable to prisoners on discharge was increased. Organised ball games were now in operation in the grounds although there were complaints that play at times could be extremely rough. During the year a number of concerts and a play had been staged. Prior to this just one concert a year was produced in which some of the best known artistes in Dublin took part. The first lecture 'Public Health' also took place in 1947.[13]

By the end of 1950 all prisoners were allowed to smoke and they could wear their own clothes. Suits were now being made in the prison. Two handball alleys had been built and the game was very popular.[14] It was in 1950 also (September) that Linda attended her last meeting. On 7 May the following year, a month before she died, the committee was informed of her illness. She had been a visiting justice during a critical time in the development of prison facilities and her work for prisoners was possibly, with the exception of the establishment of her holiday home for nurses, the most rewarding endeavour of her many faceted career.

Chapter Eleven
Women's Industrial Development Association (W.I.D.A.)

Linda was a founder member of The Women's Industrial Development Association (W.I.D.A.) which came into being in October 1932 with Jennie Wyse Power as its first president and Miss Finn, secretary. One of its driving forces was Miss E. Somers. Subsequent presidents included Mrs. Austin Stack and Linda. The main aims of the association were to promote the purchase of Irish goods and to mount an annual Christmas fair, *Aonach na Nodlag*. The Aonach involved a display of Irish crafts and products such as tooled leather, toys, cards, embroideries, woodcuts, handweaves, and radio sets.[1]

In 1908, Arthur Griffith, Jennie Wyse Power, Alderman Tom Kelly, T.S.Cuffe and other members of Sinn Féin organised the first Aonach. It continued uninterrupted except for the years 1920-23. Writing in the *Irish Press* in December 1938, Anna Kelly outlined the origins of the industrial movement out of which grew the W.I.D.A and *Aonach na Nodlag*:

> 'The Aonach is the younger child of the Gaelic League and Sinn Féin. Like most younger sons it never inherited the property. Instead it dabbles in arts and crafts. From the establishment of the Gaelic League in 1893, sprang the modern industrial movement. The late D.P. Moran in *The Leader* gave it its first press campaign. Three years afterwards, Cork came down to brass tacks and founded the Cork Industrial Development Association. After it came the Dublin Industrial Development Association. Between them they presented Ireland's first united economic battlefront to the foreigner.'[2]

In 1934 the W.I.D.A., popularly known as the 'Widas', took over the running of *Aonach na Nodlag* in Dublin.[3] The annual general meeting of that year was attended by about eighty delegates and took place on 21 November in the Supper Room of the Mansion House. It was presided over by Jennie Wyse Power and also in attendance were Mrs Austin Stack, vice-president, and honorary secretaries, Mrs McDonald, Mrs Martin and Mrs O Sullivan and honorary treasurer, Miss Scully. Linda was present and at the end of the meeting she was elected onto the executive of the association. The treasurer's report revealed that although there was a credit balance of £53-18-11 the expense of running the association's office at 51A, Dawson Street was worrying. This figure of £250 p.a. could barely cover the cost of postage. Were it not for contributions from the area committees and also individual subscriptions the society would be unable to function effectively. Despite this gloomy picture the delegates refused to increase the membership fee from one shilling to two shillings and sixpence. Jennie Wyse Power said that if the association was to be a vibrant force a membership of one thousand in the Dublin area would have to be aimed at. She asked each member to recruit at least three other women into the association.

The A.G.M. discussed the general unavailability of Irish-made articles in shops. According to the secretaries' report this unacceptable situation was only rectified when the customer specifically asked for native products. It was up to Irishwomen to ensure that they got their rights in Dublin shops. One of the delegates, Miss Donnelly, complained that there was a regrettable lack of enterprise and initiative in the Irish fashion industry:

> 'We act in the manner of dress as if we had not a single artistic idea of our own on the subject. While we continue to accept foreign decrees as the last word, it is unreasonable to expect people to purchase home manufactured garments which are only an imitation of the foreign article.'

However her motion, which had the support of Jennie Wyse Power, that 'we decree our own fashions and conventions' was lost. Motions which were passed included one to advocate the use of turf as a domestic fuel as far as possible and another to support cottage industries. A list of craftsmen was to be compiled with a view to their being assisted by the W.I.D.A.

The president reported that among the complaints received by the office was one that claimed that a brand of stockings which should retail at five shillings and sixpence was actually on sale in the shops at sixteen shillings and eleven pence. This matter had been referred to the Prices' Commission whose advice was that if an individual had a grievance she should submit it to them for investigation.

The delegates discussed at length the rates of pay for women in Dublin factories, a subject which was raised by Mrs. McMahon who said that the wages were as low as nine shillings and sixpence and even seven shillings and sixpence per week. In her opinion, 'this was a criminal state of affairs which as a women's organisation they should not countenance for a moment.' The meeting decided that the W.I.D.A. would advocate Trade Union rates only. Another delegate, Mrs Cullen, remarked that responsibility for the minimum wages in the clothing trade lay with the government.

The following delegates were elected onto the new executive: Mrs. Ruttledge, Mrs. Shanley, Mrs. O Sullivan, Miss McGeehan, MrsMcLoughlin, Mrs Scully, Mrs Corish, Mrs Martin, Mrs. McGinley, Miss Rock, Mrs. O Connor, Mrs Duffy, Miss McNee, Mrs Murphy, Mrs Connor, Mrs Dowling, Mrs Shanley, Mrs McGinley, Mrs. Dowling, Mrs Childers, Miss Barton, Mrs Ryan, Mrs McCullough, Miss Geoghegan, Mrs. McAuley, Miss McDonald, Mrs Doody, Mrs Foley.[4]

Aonach na Nodlag the following month (7-14) December was officially opened by Margaret Pearse, sister of the executed 1916 brothers, Padraig and Willie. Miss Pearse commented that she couldn't understand 'the mentality of people who have suffered for Ireland and who still do not insist on buying Irish goods. Another speaker, Rev Dom Sweetman O.S.B. castigated the banks for investing in Irish manufactures. In his opinion, 'banks were the entire cause of all the misery in Ireland.'[5]

The first branch of the W.I.D.A. outside Dublin was established in Cork in 1934 through the efforts of Leslie Barry, Mrs. F Healy and Mrs S Hegarty. The Cork *Aonach na Nodlag* of that year was opened by the minister for local government, Seán T Ó Ceallaigh.[6] By the end of 1935 the W.I.D.A. had branches in Carrigtwohill, Middleton, Tralee, Listowel, Killorglin, Dingle, Killarney and also in Cos. Clare, Galway, Limerick and Wicklow. It was proposed at the 1935 Dublin A.G.M. that the branches outside the capital be given representation on the executive thereby making the W.I.D.A. a national institution.[7]

The Women's Industrial Development Association was one of the women's organisations which voiced strong opposition to the *Conditions of Employment Bill* introduced by the Minister for Industry and Commerce, Seán Lemass in 1935. There was particular concern over section 16 which gave the minister power over the number of women employed in some areas of employment. At the first meeting of the newly elected executive which Linda attended, it was stated that similar legislation did not exist in any other democratic country and 'because experience and example are not there to guide the government, care should be taken to keep the democratic principles in establishing the conditions which all desire to see in industrial employment.' In regard to section 16 the following resolution was passed by the meeting:

> 'Believing that justice and democratic principles demand that the opportunities of women in the labour market should not be arbitrarily restricted, (the meeting) protests against the bestowal of absolute power in this respect on a minister by article 16 of the *Conditions of Employment Bill*.' [8]

Linda was now in the unusual position of being on the Fianna Fáil executive while at the same time opposed to this bill. The incongruity of her stance is highlighted by the fact that a few weeks previously she was one of the main organisers of the annual Fianna Fáil céilí, described as 'the biggest function of the kind held in the city' which took place in the Mansion House. Her great friend Dorothy Macardle also found herself in the same position as did Kathleen Clarke, widow of the 1916 leader Tom Clarke. Indeed while Linda was being re-elected to the Committee of Fifteen at the Ard-Fheis on 2 December, (1935) members of the Irish Women's Workers Union, whose driving force was Louie Bennett, were distributing leaflets protesting against the bill outside the Mansion House.[9]

Both Linda and Dorothy were also members of the National Council of Women in Ireland which was founded in 1924 to promote joint action among women's organisations in Ireland. It was affiliated to the International Council of Women in Brussels. In late 1935 the Council set up a committee to investigate legislation affecting women. Louie Bennett was chairwoman and Dorothy Macardle, vice-chairwoman. Linda and Hanna Sheehy Skeffington were also members of this committee.[10] Several meetings were held to protest against the bill. At one of these, Dorothy said that the Easter Week men had promised equality of citizenship. 'For a time all promised well. Women were freely allowed to take their share in the dangers and sacrifices of that period.' She asserted that although no conscious prejudice against women existed, there was a profound, unconscious tendency to ignore women inherent in the mentality of Irish men and this attitude was apparent not alone in the economic system but also in economic legislation. At another meeting also organised by the National Council of Women of Ireland, an English social worker, Mrs Laughton Matthews, President of the St. Joans's Catholic Social and Political Alliance said:

'We want complete equality of opportunity, pay and treatment as between men and women. Women should be treated as human beings and should not have to suffer ridiculous restrictions such as compulsory retirement on marriage in the Civil Service and the training profession. If a woman's place is in the home, she will naturally consider all the circumstances and will stay in the home but she should be allowed to make the decision.'

She claimed that the Bill was a grave menace to the free choice of any individual to select a career and was an attack on the rights of the individual. Another speaker, Professor R.W. Ditchburn declared that a claim for economic equality between men and women must of necessity be joined with a claim for economic equality for all, and the abandonment of wide differences in wealth which created different classes. At the same meeting Archie Heron, who was married to a daughter of the 1916 leader James Connolly, said that the apathy of women in regard to public affairs and matters of social and economic importance was probably more to blame than any conscious effort on the part of men to deprive women of their full place in the life of the country.[11]

In 1938, during Linda's presidency of the W.I.D.A., the women's organisation, Mná na Poblachta (Women of the Republic), in a statement issued to the press voiced their reason for withdrawing their support from the annual Aonach: 'Mná na Poblachta, Dublin, have notified the W.I.D.A. of their decision not to be associated with this year's Aonach na Nodlag, as a mark of Republican resentment at the action of that Association in inviting a Minister of the British Crown to open the Aonach.' The minister in question was Seán Lemass. In reply to the statement Linda said that the W.I.D.A. was non-political in the sense that they welcomed persons of all shades of political thought. Anybody who applied for space at the Aonach would be dealt with without regard to their political opinions. In her opinion the W.I.D.A. was one platform on which women of every political opinion could unite to advance the good of the country.[12]

Mná na Poblachta was a breakaway group from Cumann na mBan. It was formed in 1933 when a majority of members of Cumann na mBan decided to alter their constitution. The leading lights in Mná na Poblachta were Mary MacSwiney, Albinia Broderick (Gobnait Ní Bhruadair) and Nóinín Brugha, daughter of Cathal.[13]

In November 1938 Linda in her capacity of President of the W.I.D.A . in Dublin, officially opened the fifth annual Aonach in the City Hall, Cork and delivered the keynote address. Mrs. D.J. Lynch, President of the Cork branch chaired the proceedings. Also present on the platform was the Mayor of Cork, James Hickey, Rev. Dr. Bastible, Dean of Residence U.C.C., Mrs D. O'Brien, Mrs O'Sullivan and Miss K. Hayes. An apology for inability to attend was received from Bishop Cohalan. Linda began her speech by saying that this was her first visit to Cork since 1922 'when I was then honoured by being sent here on an important mission.' Since that time the aspect of national life which had made greatest progress was industrial development. This progress was most evident since the passing of the *Control of Manufacturers Act 1932* and other measures of the Fianna Fáil government to protect the native industries. Industrialists had taken advantage of that protection. Linda emphasised that women had a vital role to play in the nation's economic development:

> 'We have got to overcome an extraordinary, unnatural prejudice against Irish-made goods. If one single Irish industry producing articles which women wear has to close down, that building should be kept as a monument to show the lack of nationality in Irish women, because it requires nationality – some people call it patriotism, ... to surmount these obstacles. We all say Mr. McEntee is the Minister for Finance in this country but the real ministers for finance are the women. ... The man of the house pays the rent and rates, and he buys and pays for his own clothes, but the rest is spent by the woman of the house, and does she say every time she spends, "This money was earned in Ireland; I must keep it

here"– I am afraid not... Attempts have been made to induce the general public to use as far as possible Irish-made goods and to dress in Irish-made clothes. These appeals have in the main fallen on heedless ears.'

She admitted that the influence of foreign fashions was deeply ingrained in Irish life and that it would take united action on the part of public representatives, teachers and the educated class generally to counteract this influence. People had spoken for twenty years on the value of Irish freedom – now were they going to allow the profit of that freedom to be accumulated by the foreigner, she asked.

Linda concluded her speech with an appeal for increased membership of the W.I.D.A. The only requirement for acceptance was a pledge to buy Irish-made goods. She particularly appealed to people to buy Christmas gifts of Irish manufacture, an attractive array of which was on display on the Aonach stalls. Mrs Tadhg Donovan proposed and Cáit Ní Riain seconded the vote of thanks.[14]

The following March, Linda chaired a debate organised by the W.I.D.A. involving James Dillon T.D. and P.L. McEvoy on the subject- The Land v. Industry. The debate which was marked by banter and good humour took place in the Gresham Hotel. Linda 'refereed the match and swapped cigarettes impartially.' Anna Kelly of the *Irish Press* had this to say of the protagonists:

> 'Mr. Dillon is shortish, just a little stocky, well-nourished, pink-skinned, smooth, with a jaw he makes pugnacious by continually thrusting it forth. As an orator he flourishes the humanities. He has the voice that goes with a monocle (he should wear one) except when he talks of the wrongs of Ballaghadereen and then his Connaught accent cannot be restrained. He loves himself. He loves getting up to talk. He loves being a lonely protagonist.
>
> Mr. McEvoy is lean, long, thin, palefaced and he believes

in statistics. He represents the Federation of Irish Manufacturers, edits a Blue Book called *'The Irish Industrial Year Book'* and generally carries the torch for the industrialists. He can hurl at you at a moment's notice, figures of imports and exports, and gross totals and turnovers and values and things like that.

Dillon asserted that Irish emigration could not be accurately described as a flight from the land but a flight from economic conditions. At one point, he addressed the audience (mostly women) directly: 'If you ladies spent the day bakin' and boilin' for pigs and mixin' for fowl, you'd want more than one visit to the beauty parlour.'

Keeping up the light-hearted tone of the proceedings Mrs. Dinny McCullough said that it used to be the dearest wish of her life that a farmer's son would propose to her but she was carried off by a musical instrument manufacturer and she now 'lives in semi-detached mediocrity.'

On a more serious note Linda regretted the decline in interest in Irish goods. This had not been the case twenty years before, she said.[15]

In April, 1940, Linda delivered a lecture entitled *Women's Place in the Irish Industrial Revival* under the auspices of the National Agricultural and Industrial Association. She said that £12 million was spent annually by women on imported clothes which was a sad commentary on their patriotism:

> 'Women must not allow themselves to be satisfied with home duties. We must join and work for the safeguarding of our industries. Spend every penny you can on Irish-made goods, Irish holidays and never mind the rainy day.'

Only five industries in Ireland to her knowledge were wholly Irish-owned and administered. She regretted that Irish goods in shops were not marked *Made in Ireland* which was disappointing for the woman anxious to buy Irish. Furthermore industrialists should give a guarantee that products found to be defective would be replaced.

Mrs. Dinny McCullough in proposing a vote of thanks to Linda said that the problem lay not with women and their purchasing power but with the Irish Government that gave people the alternative to buy foreign goods. Mrs. Grace Somerville-Large, seconding, said that Irish tweeds in particular should be widely bought not out of patriotism but because they were the best on the market. She went on:

> 'Irish girls are suited for something finer than life in a factory. It should be our aim to have every country home a little factory with the members of the family the shareholders. Home industries, poultry keeping and other activities would give our women the ready money to spend wisely on the very best products and it should be our aim that these products will be Irish-made.'

Mrs J.W. O'Neill who presided over the meeting advocated the wide use of branding and advertising.[16]

The W.I.D.A. sought to showcase Irish fashion at social events such as céilithe. One such event during the presidency of Mrs. Austin Stack took place in the ballroom of the Gresham Hotel which was decorated for the occasion with gladioli and hanging baskets of pink carnations. Linda wore a gown of black taffeta with a honeysuckle design.

> 'Mrs. Stack came in a handsome black poplin gown with a note of colour introduced by a red flower. Mrs.Dinny Mc Cullough chose a smart black poplin suit and a wine poplin blouse with white dots. Mrs. R. Corish's charming gown was black moiré poplin relieved by a small black and white collar and a bunch of carnations. Mrs. M.E. Connor favoured a petrol blue frock. Her shoes of the same shade had a shamrock of Irish lace on each toe. Anna Manning selected an elegant ruby satin gown with a gold lamé sash. Dr. A. Russell was smart in a black and white striped poplin dress. Oyster parchment satin was the choice of Mrs. J Murry. Mrs. G. Reville's gown was black velvet, cut on classic lines, with a

silver trimming around the neck. Mrs J.W. O'Neill chose a lovely ivory poplin and Carrickmacross lace dress. Miss V. Gore Murphy was in jade green linen. Mrs. Seán T O'Kelly looked well in green and black poplin. Miss S Buckley's frock was of pretty gold and green linen. Miss B. Buckley wore a long graceful white linen frock. Miss Una Manning's charming white linen frock was relieved by a blue and mauve sash with shoulder straps to match. Mrs S Ó hUadhaigh looked well in jade green linen.'

Others who attended included Colonel Broy, Mr. and Mrs. B McGonigal, Mr. And Mrs. P.L. McEvoy, Dr. and Mrs. Walsh, Mrs. Kerry Reddin, Mrs Bourke-Darling, Mrs. Neilon-Walsh and Mrs. McAuley. Annie McGloin, Linda's niece was adjudged the winner in the dress competition, poplin section, with Mrs. Corish second while in the linen secton Miss Swayne was first with Linda's daughter Ann second.

In 1938 Linda was nominated to the Seanad by the W.I.D.A. on the Social and Commercial Panel. However she served for a period of just four months (April-July), failing to be re-elected in the second Seanad election in August of that year. This arose from the fact that the W.I.D.A. lost its status as a nominating body. She never really had the opportunity to get in a telling blow for the causes that were dear to her e.g. the advancement of native industry or the rights of nurses to a better pay and conditions. Her contributions were confined to voting in favour of Padraic Ó Máille in his successful attempt to be elected Leas-Chathaoirleach and to addressing the House on a motion which discussed discrimination against women's organisations:

> I think it (the motion) would be more acceptable if it suggested that the Act as it now exists might be examined with the object of including amongst the nominating bodies vocational bodies which have not the right to nominate now. For example, there is the nursing council which was established in 1919. It is a statutory body, and I think it is the best organ-

ised vocational body in Ireland today. Yet, for some reason, it has not the right to nominate. It has a membership of 16,000.

...Against that you have a veterinary vocational body with the right to nominate. It seems strange to me that the people who look after the animals of the country are regarded as being more important than the people who look after human beings... You have the Amalgamated Society of Social Services. This society of women is representative of quite a number of social service bodies. They have the right to nominate. Against that you have the Mount Street Club which has the right to nominate.[17]

The following year (1939) a vacancy arose in the Seanad with the death of Colonel Maurice Moore and both the W.I.D.A. and the Irish Nurse' Association requested that Linda be nominated in his place. In her letter to the Taoiseach, Mrs Margaret Murphy of the W.I.D.A. complained that her organisation had been deprived of its right of nomination...

'to make place for another organisation. We feel that this is a very great injustice as our organisation carries on the same activities and has a bigger membership now than at the time of recognition as a nominating body. Because of this hardship we beg to submit to you the name of Mrs Linda Kearns McWhinney as a nominee for the vacancy in the Senate... Mrs McWhinney is a very keen industrial revivalist, very active social worker and would represent the views of the large majority of Irish women.'[18]

Mary (Mollie) Feenan, president, Irish Nurses' Association, said the vacancy should be filled by Linda 'who is well known to nurses, and in fact to all Ireland. She is Hon. Secretary of the Irish Nurses' Association, Hon.Treasurer of the National Council of Trained Nurses and a member of the Nursing Council. As well as ably representing the nursing profession, which is recognised as a vocation, she would be welcomed by all Irish women as worthy of the honour of nomination by you.'[19] Linda's failure in the Senate elections in 1943 prompted Mollie to write again to de Valera:

> 'Nurses were very disappointed that Mrs. Linda Kearns McWhinney was not successful in the Senate Election, and therefore beg of you to consider her name for one of your privileged nominates to the senate. She is eminently suitable. She has devoted most of her life to national work and social services... Nurses at home and abroad would feel honoured that you have nominated Mrs. Linda Kearns McWhinney.'[20]

De Valera did not accede to the request.

Chapter Twelve

Kilrock

The mid-1940s were to prove one of the busiest and most eventful periods in Linda's life. First of all in November 1945 she began her weekly knitting and sewing column in The *Irish Press* and seven months later her holiday home for nurses was finally opened. She continued writing in The *Press* up to her final illness during which the column was written by her daughter Ann.

Everyone who knew Linda well attested to her ability as a knitter and needle woman. She learned her skills possibly at home in Cloonagh but certainly in the convent in Brussells and in Longford House where her tutor was Lady Crofton. Linda was always busy with her hands- even some holiday photos show her knitting. She was also an accomplished cook and baker although in the making of pastry she admitted she was not quite up to the standard of her sister Daisy.[1] Apart from practising her domestic skills she spent a lot of her spare time listening to the radio and she particularly liked quiz programmes. She was not a theatre or opera goer although from time to time through her political connections she received complimentary tickets to shows.

According to her daughter, Linda liked tailored clothes. She had a good dress sense and was fashionable according to her own standards. However she was not fashion conscious in the sense that she did not slavishly follow current trends.[2] Undoubtedly she was creative and innovative and there are several examples of how she could improvise in the making of a particular item of clothing. Her nephew, Séamus Mulligan, who was an officer in the Irish army, described how she turned an old tunic of his inside out and made it into a jacket for herself.[3] On another occasion by making a gown from curtain material she came to the rescue of a nurse who had nothing suitable to wear for a dress dance. When her daughter was preparing to go the Ursuline Convent in Sligo, Linda made the gym-frock from an old dress belonging to her niece Kathleen McGloin. However in this instance she experienced a real difficulty - she couldn't figure out how to make three even pleats and still have the frock the right size. She called on the assistance of Dorothy Macardle who solved the problem for her.[4]

Linda began her weekly column under the name *Penelope* on the Woman's Page of *The Irish Press* on 7 November 1945. Penelope was the famous seamstress-wife of the ancient Greek hero Odysseus and the name was chosen by Dorothy Macardle.[5] This first article was accompanied by a photograph of Linda's cousin Mary Kearns modelling a wool jumper knitted from recycled thread. Mary, who at that time resided with Linda in 29 Gardiner Place, later featured in at least two other articles.

Linda's patterns were wide-ranging. She designed for men and women and also for children. Twin sets, jerkins, cardigans, jumpers, hats, caps and even tea-cosies all featured in her articles. Her clothes for women were designed to enhance the female figure and in many instances the patterns were quite complex. It is interesting to note that one of her designs displayed a motif of the Walt Disney cartoon character Bambi.[6] Some of the models were well known and these were always named. They included Betty Whelan,[7] Florence O'Shaugnessey,[8] Peggy Cullen,[9] the actress Louise Studley[10] and participants in the 'Dawn Beauty Competition' such as Dympna Hurll,[11] Patricia O'Hara[12] and Esther O'Connor.[13] Others such as some of the nurses in no. 29 or Linda's relations Mary Kearns, Séamus Clarke or Séamus Mulligan were not identified by name.

The *Penelope* article of 24 January 1947, which featured an unnamed model, also included the following verses written by A. MacLochlainn. One suspects that some of the women leaders of the time might not totally agree with the sentiments expressed.

Give me a domesticated girl
Who knows the meaning of plain and purl,
Who, brows drawn in and tightly lipt,
Pores o'er the cryptological script,
Which tells her secretly which is which,
Rib or moss or cable stitch.

She murmurs low and her soft eyes burn,
'Repeat to asterisk and turn:
Twist front, work fifteen rows and then
(in brackets) K.17, P10.'
Groping her way thru' the jargon's fog,
'W.R.N. then K2 tog.
Wool thru' loop' and back and forth,
Plaining and purling for all she's worth.

Her epitaph now at the end of her days,
When she's purled all her P's and plained all her K's;
'Her soul is gone to a happier world,
Where nobody plained when they should have purled.'

On 10 December 1948 Linda wrote a short review of a book entitled *Continental Knitting* and the main point she made was that women on the continent made knitting an art and were adept at combining colour and design. Irish women, on the other hand, were expert knitters but were reluctant to experiment with new ideas even though no fabric lent itself so well to colour and design as knitting.

No doubt the *Penelope* column afforded Linda an outlet for her artistic flair and gave her immense satisfaction but it surely took second place to the greatest ambition of her life, an ambition which was realized when Kilrock Nurses' Convalescent and Holiday Home was opened in Howth on Saturday, 1 June, 1946, by Dr. F.C Ward, parliamentary secretary to the Minister for Local Government and Public Health. It had taken eight years of planning, coaxing and cajoling to bring to fruition what was to be the last great enterprise of her life. Initially she was of the opinion that the necessary finance could be raised without government assistance but soon found that this was impossible. Even with government involvement progress was painfully slow for as she explained herself 'no sooner had I convinced one departmental head of the necessity of such a scheme than he was changed and the same old story had to be retold to his successor.'

Official invitations were issued for the function at which the guests were treated to afternoon tea.[14] Among those who attended were Linda's nephew Bernard McGarry and her niece Annie McGloin a nurse in Baggot Street hospital. McGarry, a solicitor, was Linda's legal adviser. Dr. Kerry Reddin, chairman of the proceedings introduced Dr. Ward who commenced his speech with an outline of the history of the project. The first official move was made in November 1938 when 'Mrs McWhinney wrote to the Minister for Local Government and Public Health applying for a grant of £20,000 from the Hospitals' Trust to buy, furnish equip and maintain a convalescent home for trained nurses.' It was emphasised in the application that many nurses were engaged in private nursing and therefore in many cases were not permanently employed. Almost all these nurses were not insured and the question of provision for illness was an ever-present worry. Nurses who fell ill had to pay for hospital treatment and on discharge they couldn't for financial reasons, take the necessary rest before resuming work. It was obvious that a convalescent and rest home for nurses was a serious need.

According to Dr.Ward the application for a grant was re-offered to the Hospitals' commission who in their report of March 1939 recommended the proposal. However the project was held up because the policy at that time was to defer any proposal which was not considered of primary urgency. Furthermore the Minister found that he could not give approval for the Hospitals' Trust grant unless the project was sponsored by a legally constituted body. A company was duly formed and a certificate of incorporation was issued at the end of November 1942. The memorandum of association was in the names of: A.P. Reynolds, F. McMenamin, Henry L. Barnville, Linda McWhinney, Kerry Reddin, Patrick MacCarville, Dr. Ryan, Minister for Agriculture, Patrick McCartin, Mary Considine, Mary E. Cullen, Mary O Rourke, Honoria Kenny, Delia Thompson and John Burke.

An agreement in June 1943 provided for payments out of Hospitals' Trust funds of £8000 for the purchase and equipment of Kilrock House and grounds. A further £28,172 was allocated for endowment of the Home. The Minister was also to approve a sum to cover legal expenses and architects' and accountants' fees. The amount of the grant fell far short of the tender but 'the promoters with a tenacity that merited reward came back again and again until finally they extracted a total of over £15,000 for purchase of the property.'

Dr. Ward paid tribute to nurses and their work saying that in future planning, the nurse would play a key role and that the Minister's wish to financially assist the profession was limited only 'by the urgency of the other pressing demands on the funds at his disposal.' Rev. P. Clarke, Howth, proposed a vote of thanks to Dr. Ward. Dr. Kerry Reddin said he hoped that Kilrock marked the beginning of an effort to ameliorate the conditions of nurses all over Ireland. Linda herself remarked that this new venture had set a headline since no other country had yet provided a home for nurses. 'Our next goal must be a pensions' scheme', she added.[15]

Linda had called on many of her friends and acquaintances, particularly in the business world, to help furnish Kilrock. Among items she received either as gifts or at reduced rates were furniture, kitchen utensils, carpets and mattresses. Clerys of O'Connell Street and ODearest Mattresses were among the firms which responded to requests.[16]

Kilrock House, which overlooked Howth harbour, Lambay Island and Ireland's Eye, was available to nurses at 30/- weekly. It had a full time manageress who had previous experience in Biarritz, Spain and in a number of Irish hotels. In an interview with an *Irish Press* reporter six weeks after the home was officially opened, Linda said that Kilrock had the distinction of being the only property in the Howth peninsula entirely free of ground rent and that this freedom had been ceded to its original owner and builder, ex-Chief Justice Fitzgibbon by the St. Lawrence family. On the ground floor of the house, three furnished lounges were divided from each other by folding doors which could be opened as one large room when functions such as dances and card games were organised. The dining room and a large sun parlour were also on the ground floor. Afternoon tea was served in the sun parlour which was furnished with blue wicker chairs and matching glass-topped tables. There were eight bathrooms and all the bedrooms had hand-basins with hot and cold water. Another room was fully equipped for washing and ironing. Attached to the building was a turfhouse and a greenhouse which in July 1946 was 'full of tomatoes.' The house had accommodation for twenty nurses although upwards of fifty people could avail of the recreational facilities which included lawn and table tennis, rowing, swimming and walking in the beautiful six-acre grounds.[17]

Every effort was made to make Kilrock 'a home from home.' The nurses did not have to rise at a particular time. In fact they could stay in bed all day if they wished. Breakfast in bed became an established custom though not a rule. A nurse could invite her friends for a meal or to spend the day and should she wish she could have a private party in one of the lounges. Since her own days in Baggot Street Hospital as a young woman, Linda fully understood the isolation and loneliness experienced by nurses from the country whose time off was not long enough to allow them to return home. She expanded on this to Petronella O'Flanagan of the *Irish Independent* in February 1948.

'According to new regulations nurses work a 48 hour week and are entitled to two free days a fortnight. For nurses working in the city whose homes are in the country two days is too short a period to warrant the expense and waste of time making a journey home; but on the other hand two free days spent in hospital surroundings cannot possibly be regarded as a real break. In order to be of benefit to as great a number as possible it was decided that this home should be situated somewhere around Dublin, if possible near the sea and at the same time within easy reach of city shopping and amusement centres. It also had to be a fairly large house yet not large enough to have any kind of institutional atmosphere.'[18]

1946 also saw the death of Linda's fellow fundraiser of many years before, Hanna Sheehy Skeffington. She was buried in Glasnevin cemetery. Linda attended the funeral, at which in accordance with Hanna's wishes, there was no religious ceremony. The mourners numbered about thirty. Linda who, although not a particularly religious woman, found the burial very cold and impersonal. She warned her daughter that there would have to be a ceremony when her time came![19]

Linda died in Kilrock on 5 June, 1951 of the form of cancer called sarcoma. She had taken to her bed a fortnight before fully aware that the illness was terminal. Her daughter Ann an Arts student in U.C.D. was also staying in Kilrock at this time:

'I had just got a request for my B.A. exam fees– that would have been on Saturday 2 June. My mother sent for Madeleine O'Gorman the manageress of Kilrock and said– "I want you to do me a favour Madeleine dear. Here is a cheque. Please change it for me. I need the cash." Madeleine gave her the cash which I delivered to the university. "But", she added to Madeleine, "be sure to send it to the bank first thing on Monday– otherwise there will be trouble cashing it; it might be too late".'

Linda remained conscious to the end. She was visited

by a number of friends and politicians, including P J Burke T.D.

A couple of weeks before she died Linda told her daughter that she hoped she would wear the tiny replica of the Florence Nightingale medal in her memory. She added, 'and I want you to promise you'll never forget you are the daughter of a soldier.' According to Ann; 'she was prouder of that than anything else.'

On the evening of the removal, Ann, accompanied by her godmother, Dorothy Macardle left Creevagh, Dundrum, Dorothy's residence for the arrival of the remains at the Pro-Cathedral.

'When the hearse stopped the undertakers moved to the rear and I distinctly heard a man's voice call "Kerrymen forward!" and six men, who had obviously been waiting stepped forward and carried the coffin into the church. It was so quietly done and in such a soldier-like manner that many never even noticed. Dorothy brought me in early for the funeral the next morning. Even though she wasn't a Catholic she said "would you like to go in early?" She knelt beside me. After the mass we went out a side door.'

Wilson McWhinney, Linda's estranged husband was present at the mass but kept in the background. The President of Ireland, Seán T. O'Kelly was represented by his Aide-de-camp, Colonel Seán O'Sullivan. Prominent members of Fianna Fáil who also attended included Éamon De Valera, Seán Lemass, Frank Aiken, Gerry Boland, Tomás Ó Deirg, Seán McEntee, P.J. Little, Alderman Seán McCarthy, Lord Mayor of Cork, Seán Brady, Major Vivion De Valera, Seán Moylan, Colm Gallagher, P.J.Burke, Eugene Gilbride, Eamon Rooney, Frank Fahy and his wife, Gerald Bartley and his wife, and senators Margaret Pearse, A. Clerkin and W. Quirke.

Other groups who sent representatives were: The Fianna Fáil Executive, Kilrock Nursing Home, The Irish Nurses' Organisation, The National Council of Nurses, The Guild of Irish Catholic Nurses, The Irish Red Cross,

The Anti-Partition Association, *The Irish Press*, and various Fianna Fáil cumainn in Dublin. The funeral took place from the Pro-Cathedral to Glasnevin cemetery. The coffin was draped in the tricolour but no shots were fired over the grave. Linda was not buried in the Republican plot. According to Ann Keating 'there was some difficulty about that.'

In a tribute to Linda in *The Irish Press* Maire Comerford stressed that Linda...

> 'while engaged in the varied activities of the fight for freedom was never unaware of the human problems behind the scenes. The nurse in her understood the predicament of the men who had lost their health, of the women who must rear children on reduced means. Others could brush these things aside, but thirty years afterwards Linda Kearns still remembered and was available to do what she could.
>
> I remember the scene in some great city of the U.S.A. after a meeting at which Linda had spoken with eloquence and force. We were back in our hotel, and of the promoters of the meeting, coming to talk of the things which were in all our minds, found her darning her stockings. The repair was perfectly done. It had not occurred to him that the woman who had driven a car for the I.R.A. , who had taken full personal responsibility for the arms and ammunition in it –in order to save her comrades-- that this woman could also sew and darn. She could do more than that. She was a wonderful knitter and needlewoman, and had many other domestic and womanly skills which she perfected during the long hours of night nursing.'[20]

C O'S in *The Irish Times* wrote:

> 'As a mutual friend said yesterday "there was great stuff and quality in her" . For over 35 years she had given unstintedly of her gifts and qualities to the many causes she served. Her profession, no doubt, came first in her affection, but she shared that affection generously with her labours for the betterment of the working conditions and living of her nursing colleagues and for the attainment of republican independ-

ence for her country. Membership of the Senate for a period under Mr. Valera's regime was in some sort a token of recompense for her sacrifices in the republican struggle, though the presence and the recollections of fellow fighters of hers, at the Pro-Cathedral, might have gratified her even more... A valiant woman indeed.[21]

A year after her death, the following tribute appeared in the *Irish Press*:
'It is a year this June since Linda Kearns McWhinney died and it is difficult to realize that one will not again meet her, walking with long strides, her brown eyes alert and alive with purpose and be greeted with that wide and radiant smile.

Her eager, receptive mind made travel a joy to Linda and if there was a spice of danger in it the pleasure was enhanced. Linda seemed to know everybody and to be known everywhere. Her militant energy in a cause that she had at heart; her resourcefulness and persuasiveness; the combination of charm, humour and fearless denunciation with which she would usually achieve her ends, were forever been called upon, whether by former comrades in trouble or by the advocates of some national scheme. If her health was being worn down, her friends scarcely noticed it—there was so much fun and entertainment in her accounts of incidents and adventures; so much laughter when a battle was won. Her life, spanning the period from the eclipse of Parnell to the recognition of the Republic, was one that issued an unparalleled challenge to the sons and daughters of Ireland. From early youth to her last hours, Linda answered that challenge with all her heart.'[22]

Dorothy Macardle was the writer and it is fitting that she, Linda's closest friend should salute the qualities and achievements of this remarkable woman.

References

Chapter 1
1 Interview with Margaret Galloway (R.I.P.) 10 November 1989.
2 Interviews with Séamus Clarke, 23 September 2000 and with Damian MacGarry 25 April 2002.
3 Séamus Clarke interview, 13 April 1990.
4 Ibid.
5 Newspaper cutting from *The District Press*, 1 July 1905.
6 Parish records Skreen-Dromard parish. The baptism was performed by Fr. McNulty and the godparents were James and Catherine Kearns.
7 Interview with Ann Keating, 13, June 1992.
8 File CO 904/44, Public Record Office, London.
9 Public Record Office, Dublin.
10 Family sources
11 1911 Census, P.R.O., Dublin.
12 Newspaper cutting from *The District Press*, 1 July 1905.
13 Interview with Mary Duffy, 6 March 2002.
14 Interviews with Séamus Clarke and Damian MacGarry.
15 Interviews with Séamus Mulligan, 14 September, 1989 and with Séamus Clarke, 5 February 1994
16 Ann Keating's written account.
17 Letter dated 15 July 1951 from Louisa A. Josephs, Durham House, Thropton, Northumberland to Ann Keating.
18 File CO 904/44, P.R.O. London
19 Report of the Royal City of Dublin Hospital, 1907, Mercer's Library, Dublin
20 Letter of commendation from the Nursing Committee, Baggot Street in possession of Ann Keating.
21 Nursing Committee Minutes, Baggot Street Hospital, 8 January 1908, Mercer's Library
22 Information from Ann Keating.
23 Report of the Royal City of Dublin Hospital 1908, Mercer's Library, Dublin
24 Report of the Royal City of Dublin hospital 1900, Mercer's Library, Dublin
25 Report of the Royal City of Dublin Hospital, 1910, Mercer's Library, Dublin.
26 Testimonials in possession of Ann Keating.
27 Information from Ann Keating.
28 File CO 904/44, P.R.O., London; Nursing Committee Minutes, Baggot Street Hospital, 11 October 1911. Mercer's Library.
29 William O'Connor Morris, *Memories and Thoughts of a Life* (London

References

1895) preface. Gortnamona estate was the inspiration for the song of the same name by Percy French. Gortnamona House was burned down during the War of Independence.
30 *The King's County Chronicle*, 17 February 1916.
31 Will of Maurice Lindsey O'Connor, February 1916, P.R.O., Dublin.
32 *The King's County Chronicle*, 17 February 1916.
33 Will of Maurice Lindsey O'Connor Morris.

Chapter 2
1 Statement of Linda Kearns to the Military Archives. Copy in possession of her daughter, Ann Keating.
2 Ibid.
3 Interview with Séamus Mulligan, 14 September 1989.
4 Statement of Linda Kearns.
5 *Irish Press*, 29 November 1934.
6 Uinseann MacEoin Ed. *Survivors*, (Dublin 1980).
7 Linda Kearns' statement; Kathleen Clarke, *My Fight for Ireland's Freedom* (Dublin 1991) p 166.
8 Linda Kearns' statement.
9 Information from Damian MacGarry.
10 Interview with Séamus Mulligan, 6 November 1991.
11 File CO 904/44 P.R.O. London.
12 Interview with Vinnie Byrne, St. Nessan's Nursing Home, Howth, 16 October 1992; Uinseann MacEoin, *Survivors* (Dublin 1980) p. 322.
13 Michael Farry, *Sligo 1914-1921, A Chronicle of Conflict*, (1992) p.189.
14 Military Pension application form in possession of Ann Keating; *The Irish Press*, 2 November 1934.
15 Interview with Séamus Mulligan, 6 November 1991.
16 Interview with Mary Duffy, 6 March 2002.
17 Information from Ann Keating 4 December 2000.
18 Meda Ryan, *Michael Collins and the Women in his Life*, (Cork 1996) p.80; James Mackey, *Michael Collins, A Life*, (Edinburgh and London 1996) p.193.
19 Linda Kearns' statement.
20 Nevin Papers, War of Independence Collection, Sligo Library.
21 Linda Kearns' statement.
22 File CO 904/44, P.R.O. London.
23 Richard Abbot, *Police Casualties in Ireland,1919-1922* (Cork, 2000) p. 128; *The Sligo Champion* 2 October and 9 October 1920; *An Connachtach*, 8 October 1920.
24 Joe McGowan, *Under the Shadow of Benbulben*, (Sligo 1993)pp.113-124; Michael Farry, *A Chronicle of Conflict*, (1992) pp.253-255; Richard Abbot, *Police Casualties in Ireland* 1919-1922, (Cork 2000); *An Connachtach*, 29 October 1920; *The Sligo Champion*, 30 October 1920;

The Roscommon Herald, 30 October 1920.
25 File CO 904/44, P.R.O., London.

Chapter 3
1 Linda Kearns, *In Times of Peril, leaves from the Diary of Nurse Linda Kearns from Easter Week 1916 to Mountjoy 1921*, Edited by Annie M.P. Smithson, (Dublin 1922) p.15.
2 Linda Kearns' Statement.
3 UCD Archives, O'Malley Notebooks, File P/17b/137.Eugene Gilbride.
4 UCD Archives, O'Malley Notebooks, File P/17b/133. Tom Scanlon.
5 Linda Kearns' Statement
6 UCD Archives, O'Malley Notebooks, File P/17b/137.
7 Ibid.
8 UCD Archives, O'Malley Notebooks, File P/17b/133.
9 File CO 904/44, P.R.O. London
10 UCD Archives, O'Malley Notebooks, File P/ 17b/137.
11 Linda Kearns, *In Times of Peril*, (Dublin 1922) p.17.
12 Linda Kearns' Statement.
13 Ibid.
14 UCD Archives, O'Malley Notebooks, File P/17b/133.
15 *Roscommon Herald*, 27November 1920; *Sligo Champion*, 27 November 1920.
16 *Sligo Champion*, 4 December 1920.
17 *Sligo Champion*, 27 November 1920.
18 File CO 904/44 P.R.O., London.
19 *Sligo Champion*, 27 November 1920.
20 File CO 904/44, P.R.O. London.
21 Ibid.
22 Interview with Séamus Mulligan, 6 November 1991.

Chapter 4
1 Linda Kearns, *In Times of Peril* (1922 Dublin); Linda Kearns' Statement.
2 Ibid.
3 *Sunday Press* 10 June 1951
4 Linda Kearns, *In Times of Peril* (1922 Dublin); Linda Kearns' Statement
5 P.R.O. London, File CO 904/44
6 Sligo Co. Library,War of Independence Collection; P.R.O. London, File CO 904/44.
7 Linda Kearns, *In Times of Peril* (1922 Dublin); Linda Kearns' Statement
8 Linda Kearns' Statement; P.R.O. London, File CO 904/44.
9 P.R.O. London, File CO 904/44.
10 Ibid.
11 Ibid.

References

12 John Mulligan was married to Linda's sister Annie. They had one child, Séamus.
13 P.R.O. London, File CO 904/44.
14 Pauline Scanlan, *The Irish Nurse* (Manorhamilton 1991) p.90.
15 Interview with Margaret Vanek, Marie Mortished's daughter, 9 April 2001. Marie worked for a time in Baggot Street Hospital and may have known Linda there.
16 P.R.O. London, File CO 904/44.
17 Linda Kearns' Statement.
18 P.R.O. London, File CO 904/44; *Sligo Champion*, 9 April 1921.
19 *Sligo Champion*, 2 April 1921.
20 Linda Kearns' Statement.
21 Linda Kearns, *In Times of Peril* (1922 Dublin) p.39
22 *In Times of Peril* p.41
23 P.R.O. London, File CO 904/44
24 *In Times of Peril* p.40.
25 *In Times of Peril*, pp44-45
26 Linda Kearns' Statement.
27 P.R.O. London, File CO 904/44
28 Linda Kearns' Statement.
29 P.R.O. London, File CO 904/44
30 Ibid.
31 Linda Kearns' Statement.
32 P.R.O. London, File CO 904/44
33 Ibid.
34 *In Times of Peril*, pp 50-51.

Chapter 5

1 Linda Kearns' Statement.
2 *The Irish Independent*, 17 September 1921.
3 Linda Kearns' Statement.
4 *The Irish Independent*, 22 September 1921; Linda Kearns' Statement.
5 P.R.O. London, File Co 904/44
6 Ibid.
7 *In Times of Peril*, p.52
8 P.R.O. London, File Co 904/44
9 *In Times Of Peril* p. 52.
10 Eithne Coyle in *Survivors*, ed. Uinseann MacEoin (Dublin 1980) pp.153-54; *In Times of Peril*, pp53-58; Linda Kearns Statement.
11 Linda Kearns' Statement.
12 Ibid
13 Information from Ann Keating.
14 *The Sligo Champion*, 21 January 1922.
15 Information from Ann Keating.
16 Kit and Cyril Ó Céirín, *Women of Ireland*, (1996 Kinvara) pp.205-206;

Interview with Margaret Vanek, 9 April 2001.
17 *Irish World*, 30 September 1922
18 Article by Dorothy Macardle in *The Irish Press*, 11 June 1952.
19 Information from Ann Keating.
20 Linda Kearns' Statement.
21 Jim Maher, *Harry Boland* (1998 Cork) pp.242-244.
22 *The Irish Times* 8 June 1951.

Chapter 6
1 Memoir in possession of Ann Keating.
2 Kathleen Boland's statement. Buíochas le Annraoi Ó Beoláin.
3 Robert Briscoe, *For the Life of Me* (London 1958) pp 176-177.
4 Joe McGowan, *Under the Shadow of Benbulben* (Sligo 1993) p. 134.
5 Newspaper cutting undated and untitled.
6 *Boston American*, 27 September 1922.
7 *Boston Sunday Post*, 1 October 1922.
8 *Sligo Champion*, 26 August 1922.
9 *Boston Herald*, 2 November 1922.
10 Untitled and undated newspaper cutting.
11 *The Springfield Union*, 6 November 1922.
12 A/1035 46 (1) (A) Military Archives, Dublin. Hanna Sheehy Skeffington did not return to Ireland until the following year.
13 Robert Briscoe, *For the Life of Me* (London 1958) pp. 187-189.
14 P.80/789 Fitzgerald Papers, University College, Dublin; *Chicago American*, 22 January 1922.
15 Dorothy Macardle, *The Irish Republic* (Dublin 1999) p.811.
16 Diary of Kathleen Boland in possession of Annraoi Ó Beoláin
17 Newspaper cutting dated 27 November 1922
18 A/1035 46 (1) (A) Military Archives, Dublin.
19 Untitled and undated newspaper cutting.
20 Untitled and undated newspaper cutting.
21 Untitled and undated newspaper cutting. Date of meeting: 17 October 1922. Also *St. Paul Press*, 12 February 1923
22 *Buffalo Express*, 20 October, 1922.
23 Interview with Séamus Clarke; *Buffalo Express*, 20 October 1922.
24 The *Monitor, The Family Catholic Newspaper of New Jersey*, 24 February 1923. *The Plain Speaker*, Hazleton, PA. 11 June 1923.
25 The *Tucson Citizen*, 11 April 1923.
26 Newspaper cutting.
27 *Chicago Daily Journal*, 22 January 1922.
28 *The Tucson Citizen*, 11 April 1923.
29 Newspaper Cutting.
30 Cutting from *Los Angeles Evening Herald,* undated; Information from Séamus Clarke.
31 *Fall River Globe*, 25 June 1923.

References

32 Newspaper Cutting.
33 Untitled Carbondale Newspaper dated 9 January 1924.
34 A/1035 46 (1) (A), Military Archives, Dublin.
35 Kathleen Boland's Diary.
36 Ibid.
37 Newspaper Cutting.
38 Newspaper Cutting.
39 *The Plain Speaker*, Hazleton, PA, 11 June 1923. Linda said that $107,000 had already been sent to Ireland.
40 *Sligo Independent*, 26 April 1924; *Sinn Féin*, 3 May 1924.
41 *Sinn Féin*, 24 May 1924; Margaret Ward, *Hanna Sheehy Skeffington* A *Life* (Cork 1997), p.263.
42 Donal O'Donovan, *No More Lonely Scaffolds* (Dublin 1989), p.199.
43 In possession of Ann Keating. It is type written on rice paper, an easy material to digest in the event of capture.
44 In possession of Ann Keating.
45 *The Gympie Times*, 29 January 1925.
46 *Sinn Féin*, 16 May 1925.
47 *The Catholic Press*, 8 January 1925.
48 *The Connachtman* 3 January 1925.
49 *The Gympie Times*, 29 January 1925
50 ibid.
51 Inscription on flyleaf.
52 *The Age*, 7 February 1925.
53 The Catholic Advocate, 22 January 1925
54 untitled and undated newspaper cutting.
55 untitled and undated newspaper cutting.
56 *Sinn Féin*, 16 May and 23 May 1925.
57 *An Phoblacht*, 3 July 1925.

Chapter 7

1 Dermot Keogh, *Twentieth Century Ireland, Nation and State*, (Dublin1994), p.42.
2 Tim Pat Coogan, *De Valera Long Fellow, Long Shadow*, (1993 London) p.386; J.J. Lee, *Ireland 1912-1985*, (1989 Cambridge)
3 *An Phoblacht*, 21 May 1926.
4 Margaret Ward, *Hanna Sheehy Skeffington*, (1997 Cork) p.280.
5 Interview with Mary Duffy, 6 March 2002.
6 Information from Ann Keating.
7 Kit & Cyril Ó Céirín, *Women of Ireland*, (1996 Kinvara), p.132.
8 UCD Archives, File P176/33.
9 UCD Archives, P 176/345. Meeting of party executive 10 May 1943 chaired by de Valera
10 Interview with Séamus Mulligan, 14 September 1989.
11 UCD Archives, File, P 176/345, Meeting 24 May 1937.

12 UCD Archives, File, P 176/345, Meeting 19 April 1937
13 UCD Archives, File, P 176/345, Meeting 25 October 1937
14 UCD Archives, File, P 176/345, Meeting 8 November 1937.
15 Tim Pat Coogan, *The I.R.A.* (1970 London) p.153;
    J.J. Lee, *Ireland 1912-1985* (1989 Cambridge), p.222.
16 UCD Archives, File, P 176/345, Meeting 16 September 1940.
17 UCD Archives, File, P 176/345, Meeting 3 February 1941
18 UCD Archives, File, P 176/345, Meeting 12 December 1938
19 UCD Archives, File, P 176/345, Meeting 23 January 1939
20 UCD Archives, File, P 176/345, Meeting 10 November 1941
21 UCD Archives, File, P 176/345, Meeting 22 January 1940
22 UCD Archives, File, P 176/345, Meeting 12 January 1942
23 UCD Archives, File, P 176/345, Meeting 10 October 1938
24 UCD Archives, File, P 176/345, Meeting 8 July 1940
25 UCD Archives, File, P 176/345, Meeting 26 July 1948
26 UCD Archives, File, P 176/345, Meeting 13 September 1937
27 UCD Archives, File, P 176/345, Meeting 6 September 1937;
    Kathleen Clarke, *My Fight for Ireland's Freedom* (1991 Dublin) p.221
28 UCD Archives, File, P 176/345, Meeting 8 November 1937
29 Tim Pat Coogan, *De Valera* (1993 London) p. 500
30 Information from Ann Keating and Séamus Mulligan.

Chapter 8

1 MacEoin, Uinseann ed., *Survivors*, (Dublin, 1980), p. 163.
2 Information from Séamus Mulligan.
3 Information from Ann Keating.
4 *Sinn Féin*, 25 October 1924.
5 HA/5/1637, Public Records Office, Northern Ireland (PRONI).
6 HA/S/2478, PRONI.
7 HA/5/1637,PRONI.
8 Denise Kleinrichert, *Republican Internment* and the Prison Ship *Argenta*,(Dublin 2001), p. 19; Jim McDermott, *Northern Divisions, The Old IRA and the Belfast Pogroms 1920-22* (Belfast, 2001). p. 235; S5/750/16, National Archives (NA).
9 HA/5/1637, PRONI; Kleinrichert, *Argenta*, pp.123-24.
10 Séamus Mulligan,
11 HA/5/1637, PRONI.
12 S5/750/16, NA.
13 S5/750/16, NA.
14 HA/5/1637.
15 HA/5/1637.
16 HA/5/1637.
17 HA/5/1637.
18 HA/5/1637.
19 HA/5/1637.

References

20 HA/5/2478; HA/5/1637.
21 HA/5/1637.
22 HA/5/2478.
23 HA/5/1637
24 *Sligo Independent*,1 November 1924.
25 *Sligo Independent*, 8 November, 1924
26 *Sinn Féin*, 25 October 1924.
27 HA/5/1637.
28 *Belfast Telegraph*, 1 November 1924
29 HA/5/1637.
30 Postcards in possession of Ann Keating.
31 *An Phoblacht*, 20 July 1925.
32 Information from Ann Keating; General Register Office (GRO), Dublin, 1929 Dublin North, Vol 2 p.323.
33 Interview with Mrs. Mary Creed who was in the Richmond at the same time.
34 Interviews with Mary Duffy (née Kearns) and Sheila Clarke.
35 Interview with Sheila Clarke and Margaret Galloway.
36 Information from Séamus Mulligan.
37 Information from Ann Keating.

Chapter 9

1 Conversations with Sheila Clarke, Mary Duffy, Margaret Galloway and Mary Creed.
2 *The Irish Press*, 5 July 1933.
3 Pauline Scanlan, *The Irish Nurse*, (Manorhamilton 1991) pp.87-88.4 An Bord Altranais, Minute Books of General Nursing Council. Date of Meeting: 1 February 1934.
5 Pauline Scanlan, *The Irish Nurse*, (Manorhamilton 1991) pp.97-99.
6 General Nursing Council Minute Books. Date of Meeting:16 November 1938.
7 General Nursing Council Minute Books. Date of Meeting: 19 January 1938.
8 General Nursing Council Minute Books. Date of Meeting: 8 June 1938.
9 General Nursing Council Minute Books. Date of Meeting: 7 April 1943.
10 General Nursing Council Minute Books. Date of Meeting: 4 May 1943.
11 General Nursing Council Minute Books. Date of Meeting: 7 April 1943.
12 *Irish Nurses' Union Gazette*, July 1939.
13 *The Irish Nurses' Magazine*, March 1939.
14 Ibid.
15 *The Irish Nurses' Union Gazette*, July 1939.
16 *The Irish Nurses' Magazine*, March 1939.

17 *The Irish Nurses' Magazine*, April 1939.
18 *The Irish Nurses' Magazine*, July 1939.
19 *The Irish Nurses' Magazine*, April 1939.
20 *The Irish Nurses' Magazine*, June 1943.
21 *The Irish Nurses' Magazine*, November 1943.
22 Untitled and undated newspaper cutting.
23 Interview with Mary Duffy, 6 March 2002.
24 *The Irish Nurses' Magazine*, October 1939.
25 Red Cross Central Council Minutes. Date of meeting: 19 March 1940.
26 *Irish Red Cross Monthly Bulletin*, January 1941.
27 Ibid.
28 Tim Pat Coogan, *The I.R.A.*, (London 1970) p. 164.

Chapter 10
1 National Archives, File, Jus/ Prisons 3/ 2001/85/1
2 National Archives, File, Jus/ Prisons 3/ 2001/85/1. Date of Meeting, 6 April 1936
3 File, Jus/ Prisons 3/ 2001/85/1
4 Ibid. Date of meeting: 21 February 1938.
5 Ibid. Meeting 6 March 1939.
6 *Irish Independent*, 4 July 1936
7 File, Jus/ Prisons 3/ 2001/85/1. 4 March 1940
8 Tim Pat Coogan, *The I.R.A.* (London 1970) pp149-150.
9 File, Jus/ Prisons 3/ 2001/85/1. 18 March 1940.
10 Tim Pat Coogan, *The I.R.A.* (London 1970) p.150; File, Jus/ Prisons 3/ 2001/85/1. Annual Report for 1940.
11 File, Jus/ Prisons 3/ 2001/85/1. 17 September and 8 October 1946.
12 File, Jus/ Prisons 3/ 2001/85/1. 2 December 1946.
13 File, Jus/ Prisons 3/ 2001/85/1. Annual Report for 1947.
14 File, Jus/ Prisons 3/ 2001/85/1. Annual Reports 1949 and 1950.

Chapter 11
1 *Irish Press*, 6 December 1938.
2 Ibid.
3 *Irish Press*, 10 November 1934.
4 *The Irish Press*, 22 November 1934.
5 *The Irish Press*, 8 November 1934.
6 *Irish Press*, 26 November 1934.
7 *Irish Press*, 9 December 1935.
8 Ibid.
9 *Irish Press*, 4 December 1935.
10 With gratitude to Maria Luddy for this information.
11 *Irish Press*, 6 and 7 November 1935.
12 Newspaper Cutting untitled and undated.
13 Margaret Ward, *Unmanageable Revolutionaries*, (London 1983) pp.

References

   225-227.
14 *The Cork Examiner* 29 November 1938.
15 *Irish Press*, 25 March 1939.
16 *Irish Press*, 4 April 1940.
17 Maedhbh McNamara and Paschal Mooney, *Women in Parliament, Ireland 1918-2000* (Dublin 2000) pp. 170-172.
18 National Archives, Department of the Taoiseach Files, Ref. 4939, Cabinet File S 11338
19 National Archives, Ref. 4941 File S 11338
20 National Archives, Ref. 6135 File S 13256

Chapter 12
1 Information from Ann Keating.
2 Ibid.
3 Interview with Séamus Mulligan 4 February 1992.
4 Information from Ann Keating.
5 Ibid.
6 *The Irish Press*, 22 November 1950.
7 *The Irish Press*, 16 September 1949.
8 *The Irish Press*, 12 April 1949.
9 *The Irish Press*, 1 July 1949.
10 *The Irish Press*, 16 February 1951.
11 *The Irish Press*, 17 December 1945
12 *The Irish Press*, 24 November 1950
13 *The Irish Press*, 22 December 1950.
14 Invitation to Annie McGloin, in possession of Delia McDevitt.
15 The *Irish Press*, 3 June 1946.
16 Interview with Séamus Mulligan, 4 February 1992; and with Sheila Clarke 11 April 2001.
17 *The Irish Press*, 18 July 1946
18 *The Irish Independent*, 25 February 1948.
19 Margaret Ward, *Hanna Sheehy Skeffington* (Cork 1997) p.345; Information from Ann Keating.
20 *The Irish Press*, 8 June 1951. The writer used the initials M.C. Family sources say Máire Comerford wrote the tribute.
21 *The Irish Times*, 8 June 1951. The writer was probably Cathal O'Shannon.
22 *The Irish Press*, 11 June 1952

Bibliography

Primary Sources

National Archives, Dublin
Department of the Taoiseach Files
Mountjoy Visiting Committee, Minutes of Meetings
Will of O'Connor Morris.
1901 Census, Parish of Skreen
1911 Census, Parish of Skreen

University College Dublin, Archives
Desmond Fitzgerald Papers
Ernie O'Malley Notebooks
Fianna Fail Executive, Minutes of Meetings

Public Record Office, Belfast
Charles MacWhinney Prison File

Public Records Office, London
Linda Kearns Prison File
Linda Kearns Courtmartial File
Moneygold Informant File

An Bord Altranais, Dublin
General Nursing Council Minute Books

The Irish Red Cross, Dublin
Minute Books of Red Cross 1939-1951
Chairman's Reports

Mercer's Library, Dublin
Baggot Street Hospital Nursing Committee Records 1900-1912
Annual Reports of Baggot Street Hospital

Sligo Co. Library
War of Independence and Civil War Collection

Military Archives, Dublin
Linda Kearns Statement
Linda Kearns Letter to Annie M.P.Smithson

Bibliography

Parish of Skreen/Dromard
Register of Baptisms

General Register Office, Dublin
Register of Marriages, 1929

Material in possession of Ann Keating
Linda Kearns Scrapbook of Newspaper Cuttings mostly of American Tour.
Instruction of Eamon de Valera re. Australian Tour
I.R.P.D.F. Document re. Australian Tour.
Character References from Baggot Street Doctors
Linda Kearns Military Pension Application
Prison Correspondence of Charles McWhinney

Material in Possession of Annraoi Ó Beoláin
Kathleen Boland Diary
Kathleen Boland Statement

Newspapers
An Connachtach
An Phoblacht
Belfast Telegraph
Cork Examiner
Irish Independent
Irish Press
Irish Times
Roscommon Herald
Sinn Fein
Sligo Champion
Sligo Independent

Journals
Irish Nurses' Magazine
Irish Nurses' Journal
Irish Nurses' Union Gazette
Irish Red Cross Monthly Bulletin

Interviews and Correspondence
Ann Keating
Seamus Mulligan

Seamus Clarke
Sheila Clarke
Mary Duffy
Margaret Galloway
Margaret Vanek
Jimmy Kearns
Mary Creed

Select Bibliography

Abbot, Richard *Police Casualties in Ireland 1919-1922*, (Cork 2000)
Bardon, Jonathan *A History of Ulster* (Belfast 1993)
Briscoe, Robert *For the Life of Me* (London 1958)
Carey, Tim *Mountjoy: The Story of a Prison* (Cork 2000)
Clarke, Kathleen *My Fight for Ireland's Freedom* (Dublin 1991)
Connolly, S.J. T*he Oxford Companion to Irish History* (Oxford 1998)
Coakly, Davis. *A Short History of Royal City of Dublin Hospital* (Dublin 1995)
Coogan, Tim Pat *De Valera* (London 1991)
Coogan, Tim Pat *Michael Collins* (London 1991)
Coogan, Tim Pat *The I.R.A.* (London 1970)
Coogan, Tim Pat *Wherever Green is Worn : The Story of the Irish Diaspora* (London 2000)
Cullen, Mary and Luddy, Maria eds. *Female Activists: Irish Women and Change 1900-1960* (Dublin 2001)
Cullen Owens, Rosemary *Louie Bennett* [Radical Irish Lives Series, eds Maria Luddy and Fintan Lane (Cork 2001)]
Fallon, Charlotte H *Soul of Fire: A Biography of Mary MacSwiney* (Cork 1986)
Farmar, Tony *Ordinary Lives: Three Generations of Irish Middle Class Experience 1907, 1932, 1963* (Dublin 1995)
Farry, Michael *The Aftermath of Revolution: Sligo 1921-23;* (Dublin 2000)
Farry, Michael *Sligo 1914-1921: A Chronicle of Conflict* (Trim 1994)
Fleetwood John F. *The History of Medicine in Ireland* (Dublin 1983)
Kearns, Linda *In Times of Peril* (Dublin 1922)
Kleinrichert, Denise *Republican Internment and the Prison Ship Argenta 1922* (Dublin 2001)
Keogh, Dermot *Twentieth-Century Ireland: Nation and State* (Dublin 1994)

Lee, J.J. *Ireland 1912-1985: Politics and Society* (Cambridge 1989)
McCartan, Patrick. *With De Valera in America* (New York 1932)
McDermott, Jim *Northern Divisions: The Old IRA and the Belfast Pogroms 1920-22* (Belfast 2001)
MacEoin, Uinseann ed. *Survivors* (Dublin 1980)
McGowan, Joe. *In the Shadow of Benbulben* (Sligo 1993)
McNamara, Maedhbh and Mooney, Paschal *Women in Parliament: Ireland 1918-2000* (Dublin 2000)
McTernan, John. C *Worthies of Sligo* (Sligo 1977)
Macardle, Dorothy *The Irish Republic* (Dublin 1999)
Mackay, James *Michael Collins: A Life* (Edinburgh 1996)
Maher, Jim *Harry Boland* (Cork 1998)
O'Brien, Mark *De Valera, Fianna Fail and the Irish Press* (Dublin 2001)
O'Broin, Diarmaid *Traolach MacSuibhne* (Baile Atha Cliath 1979)
O'Ceirin, Kit and Cyril *Women of Ireland* (Kinvara 1996)
O'Dochartaigh, Tomas, *Cathal Brugha* (Baile Atha Cliath 1969)
O'Donovan, Donal *No More Lonely Scaffolds: Kevin Barry and his Time* (Dublin 1989)
O'Farrell, Padraic *Who's Who in the Irish War of Independence 1916-1921* (Cork 1980)
O'Halloran, Clare *Partition and the Limits of Irish Nationalism* (Dublin 1987)
O'Malley, Ernie, *The Singing Flame* (Dublin 1978)
O'Neill, Maire; *From Parnell to De Valera: A Biography of Jennie Wyse Power* (Dublin 1991)
O'Toole, Jimmy *Duckett of Duckett's Grove* (Carlow 1993)
Regan, John M. *The Irish Counter-Revolution 1921-1936* (Dublin 1999)
Robins, Joseph *Nursing and Midwifery in Ireland in the Twentieth Century* (Dublin 2000)
Ryan, Meda *Michael Collins and the Women in his Life* (Cork 1996)
Scanlan, Pauline *The Irish Nurse: A Study of Nursing in Ireland 1718-1981* (Manorhamilton 1991)
Taillon, Ruth *The Women of 1916* (Belfast 1996)
Townshend, Charles *Ireland :The 20th Century* (London 1999)
Ward, Margaret *Hanna Sheehy Skeffington: A Life* (Cork 1997)
Ward, Margaret *Unmanageable Revolutionaries* (London 1983)

Index

Achill, 23
Achonry, Co. Sligo, 27
Adelaide St., 37
AE, 119
Aiken, Frank, 70, 132, 163
Albany, 75
Albert St., Sligo 32,
Amalgamated Society of Social Service, 154
America, 70, 71
American Association for the Recognition of the Irish Republic, (A.A.R.I.R.), 77, 89
An Bord Altranais, 123,173
An Phoblacht, 98
Aonach na Nodlag, 143, 144, 145
Appian Way 107, 114
Argenta 108, 110, 111,115, 172
Armagh, 46
Armstrong, G.E. 109
Athenia, 132,
Atlantic City, 78,
Aughrim St., 28
Australia, 91

Baggot St. Hospital, 14-19, 129, 159, 161
Bailieboro 30
Ballacutranta, 11
Ballaghadereen,150
Ballinabole, 22
Ballinasloe, 22
Ballintrillick, 31
Ballisodare, 36, 37
Ballivor, 30
Ballyara, 27
Ballybrack, 49
Ballymote, 26, 28
Bangor Erris, 51
Banks, Joseph, 72
Barniville, Henry L., 128, 160
Barron, Capt. W.E, 52
Barry, Const. Michael 51

Barry, Kathleen, 68, 69, 92, 94, 96, 97,
Barry, Leslie, 146
Barry, Kevin, 68
Barrys Hotel, 68
Bastible, Rev Dr., 149
Bates, R. Dawson, 109, 112, 114, 115, 115-120
Beaudesert, 95
Begley, J.,115
Beirlegm, Brussells, 14
Belfast, 45, 47,48, 49, 53, 54, 55, 8, 108, 109,111, 116, 134
Belgium, 14
Belleek, 30
Belmullet, Co. Mayo, 20
Beltra, 43, 48, 83
Benbulben, 71
Bennet, Louie,147
Benson, Harry, 72
Benson, Mrs Mary, 100
Beresford Arms Hotel, 47
Biarritz, 161
Black, Seamus, 115
Black and Tans, 22, 23,38,40, 65, 72
Bloody Sunday, 41
Bofin, Ned, 28
Boland's Mills, 21
Boland, Angela, 136
Boland, Gerry, 98, 102, 103, 105,123, 163
Boland, Kathleen, 71, 77, 79, 80, 81, 84, 85, 86,89
Boland Harry, 69, 70, 81, 89
Boston, 73, 74, 82
Boundary Commission, 119
Bovevagh 107
Boyle, 30
Boyle, William, 108
Bradley, Liza, 114
Brady, Capt. Louis, 26
Brady, Dist. Inspector, 26, 27, 28

Index

Brady, Frances, 60
Brady, Kathleen, 59, 61,64, 85, 86
Brady, P.J. M.P, 26,36
Branley, Paddy, 28
Breen, Dan, 83
Brehony, Harry, 36
Brennan, Robert, 90
Briscoe, Robert, 71, 76
Brisbane, 92, 93, 94, 97
Broderick, Albinia, 149
Brooklyn, 74
Brown, Constable, 27
Browne, Mr S. K.C., 127
Browne family, 90
Brugha, NoinÍn, 149
Brugha, Cathal, 68, 69, 72,99
Brussels, 123, 124, 147
Buffalo, 77
Buncrana, 44, 45
Bundaberg, 95
Bundoran, 29
Buninadden, 26
Bunreacht na hÉireann, 105
Burke, Miss M.E., (Mary) 61,75
Burke, John, 160
Burke, P.J. T.P., 163
Burke, Tom, 31
Butler, Bernard, 103
Burke, Kathleen, 59, 62
Burke, Seamus, 61, 63, 77
Bushmills,114
Byrne, James, 116
Byrne, Monsignor, 94
Byrne, Vinnie, 23, 25,

Cahill, P. 112
Cairns, 94
Carbondale, 86
Carey, Jer, 95
Carlow, 62
Carrickmacross, 47, 152
Carrignagat, 48
Carrigtwohill, 146
Carroll, Patrick, 72
Carty, Frank, 23

Casey,Sgt. James, 29
Casey, Sgt. Michael, 50
Casement, Roger, 80, 103
Cassidy, Peter, 77
Castellini Family, 87
Cavan, Co. 30
Cawley, Thomas, 38
Ceannt, Mrs Eamonn, 21, 132
Chaffpool 26,
Chapel St., 40
Chicago, 80, 81, 82, 90
Childers, Erskine, 79, 104
Cincinnati, 85, 87
Clan na Gael, 90
Clan na Poblachta, 100
Clare, Co., 146
Clarendon St., Derry, 116
Clarke, Catherine, 11
Clarke, Constable, 30
Clarke, James, 11
Clarke, Julia, 83
Clarke, Kathleen, 100, 105, 106, 147
Clarke, Matha, 78
Clarke, Rev. P., 160
Clarke, Seamus, 157
Clarke, Thomas, 147
Clerys, 160
Cliffoney, 28, 29, 30, 31, 32
Clontarf, 107
Cohalan, Bishop, 149
Collins, Michael, 22, 23, 25, 41, 49, 59, 62, 63, 73, 74, 85
Collooney, Co. Sligo, 22, 26, 42, 48, 50, 66
Comerford, Marie,71, 86, 164
Concannon, Helena, 127
Condell, Miss E. 136
Conditions of Employment Bill, 146
Condon, P.J., 27
Conlon, Dr. P, 38, 44
Connolly's Public House, 25
Connolly, James, 148
Connolly, Michael, 66

Connor, Mrs. M.E. 152
Considine, Mary, 160
'Constable Black', 32, 34
Conroy, Bets, 122
Control of Manufacturers' Act (1932), 149
Convent of the Blessed Virgin, 14
Convent of the Cross and Passion, 63
Conway, Andy, 28, 36, 39, 46, 47, 50, 51
Cooey-Biggar, Sir Edward, 124, 125, 126
Coote, Jean, 130
Cootehill, 51
Cope, Andy, 63
Copley Plaza Hotel, 73
Corish, Mrs. R., 145, 152, 153
Corrigan, Thomas, 116
Corvin, Hugh,116
County Management Bill 1940, 103
Cork, 125, 139, 143, 146, 149, 163
Cotter, Madge, 59, 64
Cotter, Lily, 59, 64
Coyle, Eithne, 59, 65
Craig, Rev. R.S. 19
Creevagh, 163
Crehan, Fr. 30, 31
Croftons, 11, 12, 15, 156
Crowley, Kate, 59, 64
Crowley, Tadhg, 90
Crumlin Road Jail, 115, 120
Cuffe, T.S., 143
Cullen, Mary E., 160
Cullen, Mrs., 145
Cullen, Peggy, 157
Cullenswood House, 22
Cunlisk, Ann, 11,
Cumann na mBan, 22, 24, 25, 59, 67, 149
Curley, Archbishop Michael, 73
Curley, Mayor, 82
Curragh, 101

Dáil Éireann, 66, 91, 98
Daly, Madge, 22
Daly Michael, 64
Dawson Street, 59, 144
Deans Grange Cemetery, 13
Dease, Insp. 27
Dennis, C.J.,95
Deportees' Committee, 134
Derg, Lough, 47
Derry, (Londonderry) 45, 46, 104, 107, 108, 114, 116
Derry Brigade, I.R.A. 107
Derry Jail, 45, 104, 108, 111, 112, 116
Despard, Charlotte, 97
de Gann, Angela, 81
de Malahide, Lady Talbot, 132
De Valera, Eamonn, 69, 73, 74, 75, 89, 91, 98, 100, 104, 132, 155, 163, 165
Devins, Seamus, 28, 29, 31, 36, 37, 38, 44, 47, 48, 50, 51, 54,71
Devins, Willie, 28
Dillon, James, 150, 151
Dillon, Luke, 86, 89
Dillon, Wardress 61
Dingle, 146
Disney, Walt 157
Ditchburn, R.W., 148
Dominic, Fr. 61
Donnely, Miss,144
Donovan, Mrs.Tadhg, 150
Doolin, Dan, 60
Draperstown, 107
Dromahaire, Co. Leitrim, 11
Dromard, Co. Sligo 11, 17, 18, 41, 83
Druim a' Cruisha, 29
Drysdale, A.D. 109, 111
Dublin Nurses' Club,124
Duckett's Grove, 64
Dublin Castle, 33, 34, 40, 42, 53, 59
Duhig, Archbishop, 92, 94, 95,
Dundalk, 99

Index

Dundalk Jail, 70
Dundrum, 163
Dun Laoighre, 11, 13, 163
Dunne, Wardress, 61

Earlsfort Terrace, 62
Egypt, 18
Ennis, 12
Enniskillen, 116

Fallon, Dr. W., 124
Farrell, John, 38
Fawcett, Major F. 49
Federation of Irish Manufacturers, 150
Feenan, Molly, 124, 129, 154
Feeney, 51
Feeney, Dominick, 33,
Feeney, Dominick J., 33, 34,
Fleming's Hotel, 20
Flynn, Martin, 38
Fianna Eireann, 62
Fianna Fail Party, 71, 98, 99, 100, 101, 104, 105, 106, 121, 123, 143, 163
  National Executive, 100, 143, 163
  Ard Fheis, 98, 100, 101, 147
Finn, Miss, 143
Finerty, John, 76
Fisher, James, 77
Fitzgibbon, Chief Justice,161
Fitzwilliam Square, 60,
Flannery, Brian, 66
France 17, 18, 83, 112
Free State Party, 98
Frenchpark, 36
Frongoch, 21

Gaelic League, 20, 143
Galway, 30, 146
Galt, 114, 116
Gaffney, J, 77
Gaffney, Peter, 94

Gardiner Place, 20, 22, 25, 40, 69, 98, 107, 122
General Nursing Council, 123, 124, 125, 126
George, Lloyd, 40, 41, 52, 119
George V, King, 77, 96
Gilbride, Eugene, 28, 31, 36, 37, 38, 44, 46, 47, 50,51, 54, 163
Glasnevin Cemetery, 28, 162, 164
Glencar, 28, 37, 43
Glengarragh, 33
Glens of Antrim, 119
Glorvina, 12
Goff, Tommy, 83
Golden, Miss M. 75,
Gonne McBride, Maud, 97
Gore Murphy, Mrs. V, 153
Gormansotown, 33
Gorey, 63
G.P.O. 21,
Grafton St., 63
Grange. 26, 28, 30,31,33, 34
Grangegorman, 121
Green, Joseph Maxwell, 49, 51
Greenwood, Sir Hamar, 47, 53, 59
Gresham Hotel, 69, 150, 152
Griffith, Arthur, 85, 143
Grogan, Eleanor, 129,
Grogan, Thomas, 139
Groome, Joe, 104
Gympie, 95

Hackett, Dr. B.J.,60
Hackett, Mary E., 132
Halbert, Miss, 124
Hamman Hotel, 68,70
Hanley, Fr. J.J., 26
Harding, Trail, 87
Harp and Shamrock Hotel 25, 36, 43, 49
Hartnett, Peter, 73, 75
Harty, Edward, 86
Hayes, K.,149
Healy, Mrs. F.,146

Gardiner Place, 20, 22, 25, 40, 69, 98, 107, 122
General Nursing Council, 123, 124, 125, 126
George, Lloyd, 40, 41, 52, 119
George V, King, 77, 96
Gilbride, Eugene, 28, 31, 36, 37, 38, 44, 46, 47, 50,51, 54, 163
Glasnevin Cemetery, 28, 162, 164
Glencar, 28, 37, 43
Glengarragh, 33
Glens of Antrim, 119
Glorvina, 12
Goff, Tommy, 83
Golden, Miss M. 75,
Gonne McBride, Maud, 97
Gore Murphy, Mrs. V, 153
Gormansotown, 33
Gorey, 63
G.P.O. 21,
Grafton St., 63
Grange, 26, 28, 30,31,33, 34
Grangegorman, 121
Green, Joseph Maxwell, 49, 51
Greenwood, Sir Hamar, 47, 53, 59
Gresham Hotel, 69, 150, 152
Griffith, Arthur, 85, 143
Grogan, Eleanor, 129,
Grogan, Thomas, 139
Groome, Joe, 104
Gympie, 95

Hackett, Dr. B.J.,60
Hackett, Mary E., 132
Halbert, Miss, 124
Hamman Hotel, 68,70
Hanley, Fr. J.J., 26
Harding, Trail, 87
Harp and Shamrock Hotel 25, 36, 43, 49
Hartnett, Peter, 73, 75
Harty, Edward, 86
Hayes, K.,149
Healy, Mrs. F.,146
Healy, Miss, 126, 127

Index

Healy, Nellie, 129
Healy, Tim, 80
Hegarty, Mrs. S., 146
Herbert, J.A. 92
Heuston, Francis T., 17
Heron, Archie, 148
Hibernian and Foresters Halls, 41
Hickey, James, 149
Hoban, Miss, 23
Holmes, Ievers Dr., 70
Hospital Bill, 1930, 126
Hospital Sweepstakes, 126
Hospitals' Trust 159, 160
Howard, Robert 16
Howth, 158, 160,161
Houlihan, Garry, 72
Hughes, John, 74, 75
Hunt, Martin, 75
Hurll, Dympna, 157
Hyland, Molly, 23
Hymans, M., 124

Illinois, 90
Industrial Association, 143, 151
Industrial and Commercial Panel, 102
Innisfail, Queensland, 94
'In Times of Peril', 36, 38, 46, 55, 67
Ipswich, Queensland 94
Ireland's Eye, 161
Irish-America Club, 86
Irish Association of Civil Liberties, 99
Irish Guild of Catholic Nurses, 129, 164
Irish Independent, 59, 161
Irish National Association of Australia, 99
Irish Nurses' Association, 109, 123, 124, 154
Irish Nurse Magazine 129
Irish Nurses' and Midwives Union, 52, 53, 67, 126

Irish Nurses' Organisation, 67, 127, 163
Irish Pipers' Association, 96, 128
Irish Press, 99, 123, 143, 150, 156, 157, 161. 164
Irish Red Cross, 109, 131, 132, 135
'Irish Republic' (The), 99, 106
Irish Republican Prisoners' Dependants Fund, (I.R.P.D.F.), 91
Irish Times, 128, 130, 164
Irish Women's Workers' Union, 53, 147
Irish Women's Citizens Association, 130
Irwin, Sir John, 49

Jacksonville, 74
Jervis St., Hospital, 21
Josephs, Louisa, 14
Joyce, Const. Patrick, 29, 33, 50

Kean, Mrs, 78
Kearns, Annie, 13,26, 42, 66
Kearns, Beezie, (see Linda), 12
Kearns, Catherine, 13, 18
Kearns, Sarah (Daisy),13
Kearns, Julia, 13
Kearns, Kate,13, 40, 47, 5456, 59
Kearns, Mary,13
Kearns, Michael,13
Kearns, Nora, 13, 14
Kearns, Thomas, 11
Kelly, Anna, 143, 150
Kelly, Honora, 11
Kelly, J.J. 71, 86
Kelly, 'Dynamite' Mike, 76
Kelly, Tom, 143
Kennedy, S.M. 112
Kenny, Honoria, 160
Kenworthy, J.M. M.P., 47
Keogh, Aileen, 59, 61, 62,65
Keown, Const. Patrick, 29, 30
Kilcullen, 63, 64

Kilkeel, 116
Kilkenny Jail, 64
Killala, Co. Mayo, 12
Killarney, 119, 146
Killorglin, 146
Killoughey Graveyard, 19
Kilrock, 156, 158, 160, 161,162, 163
Kilroys, 22
Kirwan's, 122
Kirwan, M.J., 94

Lancashire, 114, 118
Laffey, Constable Patrick, 29, 30
Lambay Island, 161
Langan, Tommy, 74
Lardner, James B.L., 49, 50
Larne, 108,111,114
La Scala Theatre, Dublin, 98
Lavery, Cecil, 49
League of Nations, 98
Lemass, Sean, 98, 99, 115, 146, 148, 163
Leitrim, 11, 26, 121, 134
Leslie, Dr. M.F., 114
Lexington, Theatre, 72
Limerick, 90, 146
Lisconny, 26, 42, 43, 48, 66
Listowel, 64, 146
Little, P.J., 104, 163
Liverpool, 55, 57, 104, 107
Liverpool Anti-Partition Organisation, 164
Local Security Force, (L.S.F.), 134
Loftus, James, E. 86
London, 53, 71, 93, 101, 104
Longford, 23
Longford House, 11, 12, 15, 156
Lough Gill, 36, 37,
Lynch, Constable Patrick, 29, 30
Lynch, Liam, 82, 83
Lynch, Mrs. D.J., 149
Lynn, District Inspector, 113
Lynn, Kathleen, 100

MacArdle, Thomas, KBE, 99
MacAuley, 132
MacCallum Maude, 53
MacCarville, Dr. P., 110, 117, 124, 128, 132, 160
MacCurtain, Thomas, 138, 139
MacDiarmada, Sean, 21, 89
MacEntee, 128
MacLochlainn, A., 157
MacNaughten, Malcom, 114, 116
MacNeill, Brian, 72
MacSwiney, Mary, 77, 78,89, 90, 99, 114, 115, 149
MacSwiney, Muriel, 68, 69, 70, 71, 72, 74,75, 76
MacSwiney, Terence, 28, 77
MacWhorter, Mary, 81
MacWhinney James, 107
MacWhinney, Arthur W.,107
MacWhinney, Charles Wilson, 107-122, 165
McAdam, Eily, 46
McBride, Cassie, 114
McBride, Maude Gonne, 97, 139
McCabe, Alec, 22, 23, 24
McCartin, Patrick, 160
McCarthy, Dr., 121
McCarthy, Mrs Barbara, 75
McCormack, Const. John, 29, 50
McCormack, Hugh, 116, 120
McCormack, John, 74,
McCormack, Michael, 108
McCormack, Mr., 94
McCullough, Agnes, 135, 135,
McCullough, Mrs Dinny, 151, 152
McDevitt, Joe, (Prof.) 32, 33, 38,39, 45, 54
McDonagh, Thomas, 20
McDonald, Mrs.,144
McEntee, Seán, 104,129, 148, 163
McEvoy, P.L., 150, 153
McGann, John, 66
McGarrity, Joseph, 88
McGarry, Bernard, 159
McGloin, Annie, 153, 159

Index

McGloin, Kathleen, 121, 157
McGrane, Eileen, 57, 59,61,64
McGrath, Patrick, 102
McGuire, James, 82
McKeown, Fr. 47
McKinney, T.J. 132,
McLachlin, P.A. 94,
McLafferty, Dr. 63
McLoughlin, Const. Thos, 51
McLoughlin, Edward, 66
McLoughlin-Scannell, Francis, 121
McMahon, Mrs., 145
McMenamin, F.,160
McNulty, Rev. Patrick, 17
McSweeney, Leo, 82
Macardle, Dorothy, 98, 106, 121, 147, 157, 163, 165
Macardle, Sir Thomas, 99
Mackay, 94
Macready, General, 57
Madden, J.L. 74
Magill, Bessie Wilson, 107
Mainwairing, Mrs, 100
Mall (The) Sligo, 25
Mallin cumann, Michael, 103
Maloney, Kathleen, (nee, Barry), 91
Manning, Anna, 152
Manning, Una, 152
Mannix, Archbishop, 93, 96, 97
Manorhamilton, 134
Mansion House, 134, 144, 147
Market Cross, 40
Markievcz, Madame, 22, 55, 69, 90, 98, 99, 115
Marron, 23, 36
Martin, Dr., 30
Martin, Mrs. 144
Maryborough, 95
Mater Hosptial, 21, 69, 70
Matthews, Mrs. Laughton, 147
Meath Hospital, 63
Melbourne, 93, 97
Middleton, 146

Military Service Act 1934, 24
Military Pensions Act, 91
Moffatt, Ned, 32, 33
Moloney, Helena, 132, 135
Monaghan, Co., 103
Monaghan, Thomas, J. 86
Moneygold, 28, 32, 34, 38, 48, 50
Monroe,C.A. 60
Montana, 87
Moore, Colonel Maurice, 154
Moore St., 21, 22
Moore, Wardress, 58
Moran, D.P. 143
Morgan, Lady, 12
Moroney, Tim, 95
Morrison Hotel, Chicago, 81
Mortished, Mrs Marie, 52, 53, 57, 58,
Mortished, R.J. P. 52
Mountjoy Prison 24, 33, 34, 47, 57, 58, 59, 60, 64, 67, 78, 123, 136-142
Mountjoy Sq., 20
Mount Morgan, Queensland, 94
Mount Pleasant, 17
Mount Street Club 154
Moylan, Sean, 86, 163
Mulcahy, D.A., 90
Mulcahy, D. 95
Mulcahy, Richard, 80
Muldowney, 12
Mullan, Mr. 94
Mulligan Annie, (see Kearns), 42, 66
Mulligan, John, 48, 51, 107
Mulligan, Seamus, 25, 43, 156, 157
Municipal Technical School, Derry, 108, 109
Murphy, Margaret, 154
Murphy, Head Constable, Timothy, ('Spud') 39, 42, 50, 51
Murricane, T.H 27
Murrin, J.L.115, 116
Murry, Mrs.,152

National Agricultural and
Industrial Association, 151
National College of Art, 103
National Council of Trained
Nurses of Ireland, 123, 154, 163
National Council of Women, 146, 147
National Pension Fund 126
Needham, Elizabeth, 75
Nevin, Michael, 25, 90
Newark, 85
New Bedford, 75
New Orleans 88
Newport, 22
Newry, 115
New South Wales, 91, 96
New York, 64, 72, 74, 76, 77, 82, 86, 88
Neylon, Chief Inspector, 32, 33, 41, 42, 43, 53
Nĺ Bhruadair, Gobnait, 149
Nightingale, Florence, 134
Ní Riain, Cáit 150,
Nix, Kathleen, 128, 129, 162
North Great George's St., 20
North Strand, 122, 134
Nurses and Midwives Pensions Bill, 1935, 126, 127
Nurses Registration (Ireland Act), 1919, 124

Oates, Michael, 33, 34, 35
O'Brien, Mrs.D., 149
O Ceallaigh Seán T, (see O'Kelly), 90, 127, 129, 136
Ó Conaire, Padraic, 118, 122
O'Connell, Kate (nee Kearns), 40, 54, 56
O'Connell, Kathleen, 100
O'Connell, Jack, 40
O'Connell, T.J. 132
Ó Conchubair, Art, 91
O'Connor, Art, 69
O'Connor, Esther, 157
O'Connor, Joseph, 58, 61,62,63

O'Connor Morris, Gertrude, 18
O'Connor Morris, Maurice Lindsey, 17, 18, 19, 20, 23, 49
O'Connor Morris, William, 17
O'Connor, Rory, 67
O'Connor, Thomas, 74
Odearest 160
Odysseus, 157
O'Donovan, Dr. J.M. 124
O'Donovan, Sean, 105
Offences Against the State Act 1939, 102
O'Flanagan, Petronella, 161
O'Flanagan, Rev. Michael, 71, 85, 66
O'Flynn, Fr., 95
Óglaigh na hÉireann, 24
O'Gorman, Madeline, 162
O'Hara, Constable, 26, 27
O'Hara, Patricia 157
O'Hart, Dr., 28
O'Hegarty Diarmuid, 22, 49
O'Hegarty, Patrick J., 73
O'Kelly, Sean T. , 126, 129, 163
O'Kelly, Mrs. S.T., 153
Ó hUadhaigh Mrs.S., 152
Ó hUadhaigh Sean, 128
Olyphant, 86
O'Mahoney, John, 21
Ó Máille, Padraic, 105, 153
O'Neill, Mrs.J.W., 152, 153
O'Rahilly, The, 21
O'Rahilly, Miss 76
O'Rahilly, Mrs Elgin 138
O'Reilly, Bernard Joseph, 51
O'Rourke, Const. 29
O'Rourke, Mary
O'Rourke, Miss, 62
O'Shannon, Cathal 69, 164
O'Shaughnessy, Florence, 157
O'Sullivan, Colonel Sean, 163
O'Sullivan, Dr., 138
O'Sullivan, Jerome, 140
O'Sullivan. Mrs., 149
Ormonde Quay, 121

Index

Overend, Miss, 132
Owenson, Sydney (see Lady Morgan), 11

Paris, 74, 123, 124
Parnell St., 22, 122
Parnell Square, 23, 134
Pearse, Margaret, 86, 98, 101, 127, 145, 163
Pearse, Padraig, 145
Pearse, Willie, 145
Penelope, 157,
Perry, Sgt. Patrick, 29, 30, 33
Phelan, Joseph, P. 84
Phibsboro, 25
Philadelphia, 77, 85, 89
Pilkington, Billy, 23, 26, 28, 29, 32, 71
Port Royal, 11
Powerscourt, Viscountess, 132
Prince's St., 98
Providence, 85

Queensland, 90- 97
Quigley, Mark, 66
Quinn, Hill, Sara, 88
Quinn, Jennie H, 78
Quinn, Miss, 20
Quirke, W., 163

Ranelagh, 22, 23, 122
Raughley, 44
Reconstruction Committee,
Reddin, Christopher, E. 139
Reddin, Dr. Kerry, 128, 159, 160
Reddin, Mrs Kerry, 153
Rennick, Const. Edward, 51
Reville, Mrs. G., 153
Reynolds, A.P., 160
Richmond Hospital, 122
Riverstown, 48, 66
Robinson, 12
Robinson, D.L. 132
Roche, Det. Officer, 138
Rochester, 82

Rockhampton, 94
Roscommon, 17, 82
Roscommon Herald, 31
Rosses Point, 28
Rourke, Const. Michael, 29, 50
Russell, Dr. A., 152
Russell, District Inspector, 26, 27, 32, 34, 42, 43, 53
Ryan, Dr, 160
Ryan, Meda, 25
Ryan, Tim, 62, 63

San Antonio, 82
San Francisco, 87
San Jose, 87
Santa Clara, 86
Sandyford Cumann, 103
Scanlon, Mrs Frank, 73, 74
Scanlon, Tomas, 36, 37, 40
Scott, Peter, 92
Scully, Miss., 144
Shaw, Major F.H. 52
Sheehy Skeffington, Hanna, 71, 75, 76, 78, 86, 90, 98, 99, 138, 147, 162
Sheehan, Archbishop, 97
Sheilds, Adolphus, 52
Sheilds, Arthur, 52
Sheilds, William Joseph (Barry Fitzgerald), 52
Shelbourne Hotel, 36
Sherwin, Frank, 103
Sinn Féin, 21, 30, 32, 66, 71, 84, 90, 98, 114, 116, 120, 143
Sligo, 11, 22-47, 66, 67, 69, 83, 100, 115, 121, 122, 156
Sligo Champion, 30, 32, 40, 41, 47, 66
Skreen, 48
Smyllie A.W.G. 70
Smithson, Annie M.P. 67,68, 76, 78, 86, 126, 131
Somers E., 143
Somerville-Large, Grace, 152
Sooey, 66
Spratt, Const. 29,

Springfield, 87
Sperrin Mountains, 108
Stack, Austin, 77
Stack, Liam, 64
Stack, Mrs. Austin, 143, 144, 152
Stephenson, E.W. 113
Stokes, Alderman, 96
Stokes, Miss, 129
St. Joan's Catholic Social and Political Alliance, 147
St. John, Canon, 55
St. Lawrence Family, 161
St. Vincent's Hospital, 24
St. John Gogarty, Oliver, 62, 63
St. Ultans, 100
Summerhill College, 37
Sweetman. Fr. , 63
Switzerland, 18
Sydney, 96, 97
Syracuse, 82

Talbot de Malahide, Lady, 132
Teeling's Monument
Theodore, Premier, 94, 97
Thomastown, 21
Thompson, Delia, 160
Timmons, Mr. E., 105
Tobin, Liam, 25
Toomey, 20
Toowomba, 94
Toppin, Henry,
Tourmakeady, 20
Torbitt, Lizzie, 114
Townsville, 94
Tralee, 146
Trinity College, Dublin, 18, 70
Tubbercurry, 26, 27, 28
Tucson, 82
Tullamore, 16, 19

Union Wood, 38
Ursuline Convent, 122, 157

Victoria, 16, 91, 96, 97
Victoria Barracks, 45, 47

Virginia, 76

Walsh, Frank, 74, 82
Walton Prison, 55-58
War of Independence, 24, 76, 80, 83, 99, 107, 123, 136, 138
Ward, Dr. F.C., 127, 158, 159,
Warwick, Australia, 95
Washington, 76, 89
Watters, Wardress, 61
Webster, Rev. J.T. 19,
Westfield, Mass., 87
Whelan, Betty, 84, 157
White, Mr. 22
Wicklow, 121, 146
Williams, J.A. 109
Wine St., Sligo, 37
'Wizard' (The), 102
Women's Industrial Development League, (W.I.D.A.) 143-154
Woods, Tony, 24
Woodlawn, Co. Galway, 30
Worcester, 78, 79
Wylie, Hon. W.E., 132
Wyse Power, Jennie, 143, 144, 145

Young, Hamilton, 116
Young, 129

Index